Praises for:

Coming Clean

As you read Bucks devotional you are being welcomed into an adventure.

In the history of Christian literature, there is one book that has been read more than any other, *other than the Bible,* and that is John Bunyan's 'Pilgrim's Progress.' Pilgrim's Progress has the virtue of being honest. It tells us that life is hard, that there are real spiritual consequences to our decisions and actions, that we need others to make it through this life, that ultimately God is the provider of all the gifts and strength we will need to make it through. Pilgrim's Progress is raw, biting, truthful, and at times even depressing as it wrestles with all the struggles, disappointments, and pitfalls of this life.

I bring Bunyan's pilgrim up because that is exactly what comes to mind as I read Buck's devotional. Honest, hard-hitting, no pretending, no obfuscating reality with sugar-coated prose. Here are the facts of our struggle, we mess up and we need help from God, and pretending otherwise will not get us anywhere. There is the added blessing of real hope in what Buck shares! There is another side that we will breakthrough to if we preserver! There is healing for the soul that is ready to do business with the living God! This is a book of daily reminders of what needs to happen if we decide that we really are ready to get well, to have peace with God, and to move on in our spiritual lives.

—**Pastor Gary B. White**, Senior pastor at Cambria Vineyard Church

***

The only way a sexually broken man can make real progress is to grow in his relationship with Jesus. That means prayer and assimilation of God's Word. Buck Levis's **Coming Clean** is a great help from men needing to connect with God through Scripture. It provides a short reading from the Bible, thoughts on how to incorporate that into your recovery, and a provocative question for further study and prayer. I recommend it, especially if you've had a hard time getting your devotional discipline off the ground.

—**Russell Willingham**, New Creation Ministries, Creator of the Breaking Free recovery curriculum

***

This book speaks difficult truths.

We ALL as human beings are flawed, in Biblical language sinful. The behaviors that grow out of this flawed nature often are ruinous and greatly destructive in our lives and the lives of others we hold dear, indeed to ever broader communities.

We cannot by our resources eliminate these flaws, help, and restoration comes only through our creator God: Father, Son and Holy Spirit. Try as we might with all the resolve we can muster, we cannot cure ourselves.

However, we can come to God for help and receive help without condemnation. This is a continuing process: to admit our helplessness and to as God for help is but the beginning of the restoration process.

—**Dr. Richard P. Whitehill**, Doctor of Psychology, retired professor at University of California San Diego, School of Medicine

***

I have known Buck Levis since the mid-1980s, about 35 years. What began as a friendship then support of our ministry work, a residential recovery/discipleship program for addicted men which I directed for 28 years, grew quickly. As Buck's position in the Court system evolved, he became a colleague who occasionally referred men to our program as an alternative sentence for drug-related offenses and regularly offered ideas and counsel to us as we worked within the judicial system.

A prayer time I was part of began to grow, and Buck was one of the first few to join with us in a group that eventually numbered nearly a hundred men seeking God. Through time spent together in prayer, counsel, and confession, our friendship developed to the point that Buck became a confidant, whom I call a mentor, and in his flowing Black Judicial Robe, joined with other ministers in officiating and conducting the vows for my marriage.

Buck has been candid with me over the years about his life struggles, and the personal agony from which this deep well of devotional insight was birthed. Therefore, as I continue to counsel men, this devotional book will become a textbook I will pass on to the men I serve as the issues addressed are "Such as is common to men"! Thank you, Buck, for your honesty and contribution to the growth and freedom of men of all ages.

—Dr. Douglas Erickson, D. Min. Founder, Embassy Ministries International

***

Coming Clean is a year of daily devotional reflections on Scripture journaled by a man during what he called "the greatest struggle of my life." The personal application of the truth of God's Word by Buck Levis is candid, insightful, honest, and direct. Although written by one who struggled with sexual sin, Buck has come to see that what was learned offers "help for all of us who plagued by a besetting sin of any kind, whether sexual or any other kind."

Reading God's Word each day, Buck asked God to pick an excerpt from Scripture and show him what that passage meant in his life at the moment. This he did for approximately four years. Grouping them "by the things in his life with which God was dealing, no attempt was made to put them in chronological order."

Such a highly personal devotional book could be viewed as somewhat limited. However, well written and truly insightful the reader will find they, too, are being enlightened and challenged, as each devotional concludes with a personal and practical question, followed by four relevant passages of Scripture.

—Dr. John Amstutz, Pastor, Missionary, Author, and professor. Founder Central Valley School of Ministry.

COMING CLEAN

(2nd Edition)

W. Kent Levis

*While the author's name remains William Kent Levis, Jr, he's been known as **Buck** since he was about 2 weeks old, to friends and family.*

FOREWORD

This devotional was written during the greatest struggle of my life. I was enmeshed in the terrible secret of sexual sin that started when I was very young. The details of my sin are not important, and it would serve no purpose to write about them.

When first writing the book, I believed its purpose to be a help for those struggling with sexual sin. That has not changed, but as I added questions and verses to the commentary, I became convinced that it offers help for all of us who are plagued by besetting sin of any kind, whether sexual or of any other kind. If you are under any persistent attack from the enemy and/or your sin nature, then I pray that this book might help you as it has helped me.

It should be noted that the book is written for those who believe in the Lord, Jesus Christ, and in His word contained in the Bible. If you have never come into a relationship with God, I would urge you to simply ask Him for forgiveness for your sin and give every bit of your life and your being to God before you begin.

For many years I would commit to myself, and to God, that I would sin no more, only to fall back into sin at the next temptation. It was not until I reached a crisis in my life that I realized that I could not overcome my sin by myself. And so, I swallowed my pride, discarded my carefully cultivated image, and sat with my brothers and allowed God to heal me. This is my journey, and I share it with you for whatever help you may find in the thoughts and words that God has given me.

During my journey, I read God's word daily and asked God to pick an excerpt from scripture and show me what that passage meant in my life at the moment. God gave me one page in my journal every day for a period of approximately four years. I have not attempted to put these in chronological order as I wrote this book, but rather, I have grouped them by the things in my life with which God was dealing.

Finally, I did not want to write this devotional, but I believe that it was, and is, God's will that I do so. In answering the inevitable condemnation of those who will judge me, please believe that no one is more critical of what I have done than I am myself. But I also believe that a man's character should be based less on what he has done than on what he has done about what he has done.

TABLE OF CONTENTS

JANUARY

JANUARY 1

Text: *Proverbs 5:14: I was almost in utter ruin in the midst of the assembly and congregation. (NASB)**

There I sat, on Sunday mornings and Wednesday nights, at men's retreats, and Bible studies, a devoted member of the church. I had made a valid and real profession of faith. I knew I had eternal life. I had been baptized and I had been going to church and studying God's word for 30 years. I loved the Lord with all my heart, and God had given me wonderful gifts. I was in the midst of the congregation, and sexual sin had me a breath away from total ruin and utter devastation--and I knew it. I was powerless to change. The enemy kept telling me that I would never change; that I was doomed to a life cycle of sin followed by repentance, followed by sin. Then God heard my plea. He sent my brothers to stand beside me, and He pulled me from the pit that I might worship in the assembly, clean, before Him.

Where does the enemy have you? Are you afraid to take God's hand?
Psalm 111:10, Psalm 139:7-10, Matthew 8:1-3, Acts 17:26-27

JANUARY 2

Text: *Proverbs 26:24: A malicious man disguises himself with his lips, but in his heart he harbors deceit.*

Some sit in the assembly and worship God with their lips, their tithes, and their service, but their eyes become distracted by the flesh and their minds fill with perversion. Such was I. Friends asked how I was, and I smiled and said "just fine," when in reality the fires of lust had consumed my soul. Because sexual sin is so shameful in our society, I learned at a very early age to cover it over, to never admit this sin to anyone, to lie easily and well. But in the end, our sin will be found out, and our shame over hidden and uncon-fessed sin is greater than the shame would have been had we admitted it, and sought forgiveness, restoration, and God's righteousness.

Does your heart match your image today?

Ephesians 4:22-25, 1 Corinthians 6:19-20, Romans 8:29-30, 1 John 4-6

JANUARY 3

Text: *Deuteronomy 29:19: When such a person hears the words of this oath, he invokes a blessing on himself and therefore thinks "I will be safe, even though I persist in going my own way."*

This passage describes a hypocrite: it describes me. I have expected God's favor and forgiveness because I performed some ritual or recited some incantation. Then I went about my business, never thinking about God, while I was frolicking with other gods that allowed me, and even encouraged me, to pander to my fleshly desires. I believed that because God had blessed me, he would never be angry with me, that my salvation was assured, and that God's mighty hand would never be set against me. But deep inside of me I knew that in His perfect justice, He could not allow this to go on. I knew that as long as I persisted in playing the fool, His mighty hand must be raised against me, even though I refused to acknowledge what I was really doing. But even as I turned away from other gods and stopped relying on formula forgiveness and came to the one true God honestly and openly, I was forgiven.

On what do you rely for protection when you are in sin?

Psalm 32:6-7, Proverbs 3:5-6, Isaiah 45:22, Acts 3:19

JANUARY 4

Text: *Numbers 32:23: But if you fail to do this, you will be sinning against the Lord; and you may be sure that your sin will find you out.*

G od says in this passage that my sin is a sin against God and is sure to be revealed. I cannot sin against God and have it remain as a private matter, because any sin against God is a public betrayal of the trust that God has placed in me and a betrayal of my salvation. Our Lord was publicly humiliated for my sin. He suffered openly before all mankind and died in public, that all eyes, for eternity, might see what God has done for me. Since the act of forgiving my sin on the cross was a public spectacle, should my sin be a private matter? I can only be free of my sin if I repent. I can only repent if I acknowledge my sin. I can only acknowledge my sin if I confess my sin to others. I am free, thanks only to what the Lord has done in the light, not in the darkness.

When you repent to whom do you confess? Do you fear man's condemnation?
James 5:16, 1 John 1:9, Romans 8:1, Luke 6:37

JANUARY 5

Text: *2 Corinthians 12:9: My grace is sufficient for you, for my power is made perfect in weakness.*

T he stronger I am, the less I need the power of the Holy Spirit to withstand the temptations of the world." When I say this, I am arrogant. The truth is that the stronger I THINK I am, the less I THINK I need the power of the Holy Spirit to withstand temptation. It is not only arrogance; it is one of the most basic forms of denial. It is the belief that, on my own, I have the strength to withstand the onslaught of the enemy who is intent upon the destruction of my soul. In the moment that I empty myself of this egotism and confess to God that I am totally incapable of resisting the temptations of my flesh, the Holy Spirit fills me and I can have victory over sin.

Do you believe that you are strong enough to withstand the temptation in your life?
Psalm 28: 6-7, Psalm 46:1, 1 Corinthians 1:25, Matthew 16: 24-25

JANUARY 6

Text: *Acts 5:4: You have not lied to men, but to God.*

And then, Ananias died. How many times have I lied to God? How many times have I confessed sin but not all of it? How many times have I repented but not turned away from my sin? How many times have I told myself that God doesn't really care, knowing full well that I was in sin, or told God that it was okay because I hadn't hurt anyone else? All these were lies, lies to God and the Holy Spirit that dwells in me. Lies to my Savior as He hangs on the cross. And yet, God does not strike me dead but rather forgives me. He has known my heart, always. I have repented of all the lies I have told to my Lord, all the lies I told to myself, and the lies I have lived in my denial. When I stand before God, there will be no surprises, for God has known me always, and I have come to dwell in his truth.

What lies do you tell yourself, and how do they affect your relationship to God?
Romans 1:24-25, John 8:32, 1 John 1: 6-7, Galatians 6:7

JANUARY 7

Text: *John 11:10: It is when he walks by night that he stumbles, for he has no light.*

It is not as if I had never seen the light, for I had. In the turning to temptation, I deliberately turned away from the light and walked into the darkness. The longer I walked the darker it got, until I could see the light no more. But of course, I wasn't looking for the light because my gaze was fixed upon the temptations. Naturally, I stumbled. I stumbled so often that after a while I could not rise again. Alone in my darkness, with no strength to stand, surrounded by the evil of my sin, I called to God and he found me, because I could not find him. I must never turn away from the light again.

> *Do you want the light to dispel the darkness?*
> *John 3:19-21, 1 John 1:7, Acts 26:18, 1 Thessalonians 5:4-5*

JANUARY 8

Text: *Jeremiah 5:12: They have lied about the Lord; they said "He will do nothing! No harm will come to us; we will never see sword or famine."*

It is, of course, the lie of the enemy. I have believed it, or at least I have convinced myself that I believed it. The lie of the enemy today is that "God is love." And surely that is true. But the enemy takes what is true and perverts it. God is love, but that is not all God is. God is not a one-dimensional being, and we are not free to ignore his commands and his righteous anger because He loves us. The truth is that the Father loves us too much not to correct us when we practice evil. He has corrected me, and it has often been hard, and He will continue to correct me and it will not be fun. Yet, I know that He loves me more than I can comprehend.

Do you believe that God loves you enough to provide correction?
Proverbs 15:10, Job 5:17, Hebrews 12:11, Revelation 3:19

JANUARY 9

Text: *Numbers 16: 1-2: Korah son of Izhar, the son of Kohath, the son of Levi, and certain Reubenites—Dathan and Abiram, sons of Eliab, and On son of Peleth—became insolent and rose up against Moses.*

The word of God says they became insolent. It is more than disobedience. It is disobedience knowing that you are in sin, while proclaiming to the world that you are not a sinner: that you are holy and as worthy of respect as those who live righteously before God. The Lord responded by wiping the insolence from the tribes of Israel, by allowing those who were insolent to become diseased and die, and the infection of insolence died with them. God did not tolerate insolence in Moses' day and He will not tolerate it today. And yet, I have been insolent before God and before the congregation. But God knew my heart and has forgiven me even this sin. I stand even now as a sinner among God's people, but a repentant sinner to whom God has shown great mercy. He has restored me to his people.

Does insolence harbor sin that you are not willing to reject?
Romans 1:32, Psalm 5:5, Jeremiah 48: 29-30, 2 Peter 2:9-10

JANUARY 10

Text: *Proverbs 30:11-12: There are those who…are pure in their own eyes and yet are not cleansed of their filth.*

We live in a world without right or wrong. If I practice something abominable, and yet convince myself it is okay, the world will agree with me. Pornography abounds. It is found on every street corner, television set, theater and computer. It is available in every city and every home with the flick of a switch. The world says it is legal. But what does God say? Would I forward that image that I downloaded from the internet to God? Would I share a pornographic magazine or book with Jesus? Would I invite the Holy Spirit to accompany me to an X-rated movie? Yet this is exactly what I do because God lives in me. Then the enemy comes in with the greater lie, that if it is okay to watch, it is okay to participate. And because it is legal, I convince myself that I'm all right, pure only in my own delusion, and caked with filth before God. God commands me, and the world, to come to Him and walk with Him in purity.

What does the world allow in your life that God condemns?
1 Corinthians 6:12-13, 1 Corinthians 10:22, Colossians 3:5, 1 Peter 2:11

JANUARY 11

Text: *Acts 2:42: Save yourselves from this corrupt generation.*

Peter's words to the first-generation Christians echo down the corridors of history. The state of the world has not improved, and in many ways it has become worse. We live in an age that has been described as practicing heaven on Sunday and living like hell the rest of the week. We have added the sin of hypocrisy to our long list of corrupt practices. But Jesus came that we might have life. I cannot change society, this nation, or the world; but I can change my world. The change, of course, comes not through my own strength but through the strength of Christ. My job, the action that I must take to save myself, is to accept that which Jesus has done and allow His power and strength to change my world. I must "save myself" by making the choice to allow Jesus to transform my life from the corruption that surrounds me to the joy of life with Him.

What is hardest for you, in this corrupt world?
John 15:19, 1 John 2:15-17, Romans 12:2, John 16:33

JANUARY 12

Text: *Acts2: 28: You have made known to me the paths of life; you will fill me with joy in your presence.*

As I wallowed in the trough of my own sin, I could look out and see the path that led away from the filth that entrapped me, but I could not find the beginning of the pathway, and besides, I loved the filth even as it repulsed me. But I did cry out to the Lord to show me the way that I might become clean. I asked the Lord that I might be cleansed and taken far away from my sin by a single touch of His hand. The Lord knew me too well for that. He knew that if it was easy for me to be cleansed, it would be easy for me to return to my sin. Instead, the Lord showed me the start of the path to purity and began to cleanse me as I walked. The sin that I committed is still there, but now I am walking away from it and no longer have to look at it.

Have you found God's path out of your sin?
Psalm 34:6, Psalm 32:8, Matthew 7:7-8, John 10:3-4

JANUARY 13

Text: *Revelation 18:7: ...for she says in her heart, "I sit as a queen and I am not a widow and will never see mourning."*

These are the words of Babylon, the queen of sin, the example of rebellion against God, the archetype of evil. And she says, "Everyone still loves me, I have power and I will live forever," even as she faces certain destruction. Have I not done the same? Confronted by my sin, facing the consequences of my own evil, I thought the same thoughts. Staring at the inevitability of discovery, the certainty of loss, the end that brings total destruction upon me, I maintained my sin, and told myself that I could control my destiny when I was totally out of control. I, too, told myself that everyone loved me just as I was and that there was no reason to change. I told myself that the pleasures of sin would last forever, even as I slid deeper into the irretrievable pit. It is the ultimate lie of the enemy as he tries to tell us that we don't need God. But God exposes the lie.

Are you in denial about your sin?

Titus 1:15-16, Romans 8:13, James 4:4, 1 John 1:10

JANUARY 14

Text: *Lamentations 3:55-56: I called on your name, O Lord, from the depths of the pit. You heard my plea: "Do not close your ears to my cry for relief."*

I was in the deepest pit of sin, the one created by the enemy who had watched me and knew where I was most vulnerable. He started with my temptations when I was very young and, as I grew, so did my sin, until I reached the point at which I was ready to give up. I had tried and tried to fight my way free from my sin. The enemy had tricked me into believing that my prayers would save me, that a heart yearning to be clean would cleanse me, that vows before God would add to my strength and resolve. But nothing I did kept me from returning to the filth of my sin. I finally called to God, and He heard me as I gave up completely and admitted to Him that I was helpless and hopeless. It was then that God began to give me strength and courage and a band of brothers to help me. But God could not hear my cry until I had exhausted every bit of my strength.

> *On what do you rely to bring you out of your sin?*
> *Psalm 37:39-40, John 1:29, Psalm 50:15, John 8:34-3*

JANUARY 15

Text: *Job 3:25: What I feared has come upon me; what I dreaded has happened to me.*

I lived with an ever-present awareness of doom. I knew that I practiced a sin that would kill the spirit within me and would bring me physically to ruin. I dreaded having to stand before God and admit to the awful sin that I was committing. I knew that no matter how deep I tried to bury it that, as I sinned, I was grieving Jesus, the Holy Spirit that He has given me, and my God. I learned to live with the dread and the belief that I would not be found worthy of Heaven, because I had trampled on the gift of God. Though I still feared the consequence of my sins, I could not run from nor elude it. It was a constant in my life. But God showed me that I could overcome the fear through true confession, real repentance, and daily walking out the freedom that He has given to me. He replaces the fear with peace.

> *Do you live in fear?*
> *1 John 4:18, Proverbs 5:22-23, 1 John 1:9, John 3:16*

JANUARY 16

Text: *Psalm 146:8: The Lord sets prisoners free, the Lord gives sight to the blind.*

I was blinded by the bright lights of the world. The overwhelming, all en-compassing, neon invitation to feed the lust of my flesh had blinded my eyes the way a flash bulb creates blindness in a darkened room. I looked for God, knowing He was there, but I could not see Him. I listened for His voice, but it was drowned out by the laughter of those who had turned their backs on God's law. I tried to come to God but found myself imprisoned in walls of flesh, unable to break free of the temptation and lust that surrounded me. But my Lord had not forgotten me, and He caused me to see again, to be free once more, because of what He has done, not because of anything that I could do. It was God's righteousness that healed me, for I have no right-eousness. He came when I gave up all I had to Him.

Is God's love and forgiveness being hidden by the world?
Isaiah 59:1-2, John 8:12, John 3:19-21, Ephesians 4:17-19

JANUARY 17

Text: *Proverbs 1:10: My son, if sinners entice you, do not give in to them.*

My sin begins with me. I allow myself to be enticed; my flesh even seeks to be enticed. My flesh calls out to my limbs and instructs me where to go, that I might have momentary satisfaction, a transitory release. My body seems to have a will of its own, unstoppable, even though my heart is crying out for purity and freedom from sin. There are those who receive me into the world with arms open wide. There are even those who seek me out to draw me into sin, for if my friend is a sinner and I do not sin with him, I am a rebuke to him, and he will try all that much harder to pull me in. I must flee; I must not give in; I must gird myself with the strength of God's love, and the power of His word, that my willing mind be not enticed by evil.

Do your friendships help you or hurt you?
2 Peter 2:18-19, 1 Corinthians 15:33, Proverbs 12:26, James 4:4

JANUARY 18

Text: *Proverbs 9:17: Stolen water is sweet; food eaten in secret is delicious.*

Most of my sin, especially sexual sin, is hidden sin. Somehow, part of the addiction is "getting away with it." Doing things in the darkness that no one knows about somehow adds to the pleasure of sin. I have sinned and gotten away with it, almost as if I were playing a game and I won. The secrecy adds to the intrigue; the intrigue adds to the excitement, and the longer I practice the dark deception, the better I get at hiding. The better I am at hiding, the more depraved I become. Stolen water—my ill-gotten sexual exploits, food eaten in secret—the sin that no one knows about, is more highly erotic precisely because it is concealed. But, of course, God knows. His eyesight is not restricted to daytime deeds. He sees what happens in the darkness. He sees it all, and He weeps over my sins. When the curse of secrecy is broken, the fruits of the light bring joy.

Are you hiding your sin from God?
Psalm 69:5, Psalm 32:3-5, Proverbs 28:13, Hebrews 4:13

JANUARY 19

Text: *Luke 15:20: But while he was still a long way off, his father saw him and was filled with compassion for him; he ran to his son, threw his arms around him and kissed him.*

S till a long way off" --does that not describe me when I am caught up in sexual sin? I had wandered into the world. I had left God's side and His protection. I had believed that God couldn't see me, and wouldn't, even if He could. But God was constantly seeking me, looking out into the distance to see if He could find me. I made a decision to abandon my sin, to repent, to become clean before God. He watched, and the moment I made that decision, He saw me, and He ran to me. He did not require me to get clean before He hugged me. He is the one that provides the cleansing and the robe. He saw me as I turned.

Can God find you?
Psalm 40:1, Acts 3:19, Acts 17:26-27, Luke 19;10

JANUARY 20

Text: *Psalm 119:139: My zeal wears me out, for my enemies ignore your words.*

L ord, I try so hard to resist the temptations of the flesh, but they flow inexorably toward me, like an overwhelming tide that leaves me powerless to resist. I watch in fascination as the wave draws near and, with each new wave, I fear that again I will be overcome, and drown in a sea of filth. I am worn out, tired of trying to stand, and tempted to submit to the tide and simply float away on a sea of selfishness. No matter what I say or do, I cannot resist the temptation. And yet, God can stop the tempting tide. His words are like sea walls that protect me from the worldly temptation. I have no strength to resist, but God's strength is above all, and He will protect me as I turn to Him.

Are you overwhelmed by the evil of the world?
1 Peter 5:8-9, James 4:7, 1 Corinthians 10:13, Psalm 97:10

JANUARY 21

Text: *Psalm 119:113: I hate double minded men, but I love your law.*

D ouble minded: being of two minds; having a foot in each camp. These expressions describe the man who cannot, or will not, commit himself to a single and solitary path. He commits his life to God, and then takes it back that he may dwell in sin when temptation offers him pleasure. It is not that he does not love God, but he also loves sin. Your word, O Lord, tells us that we cannot serve two masters and, if we do, that sooner or later one will consume the other. God has given me his law for my own benefit, to bless me, but his law is strict. It brooks no other gods. I must turn, now, from the god of flesh in my life, and give myself totally to the one and only true God and to His commands.

Is there only one God in your life?
James 4:4, Matthew 6:24, Mark 12:29-30, Exodus 20:2-3

JANUARY 22

Text: *Psalm 102: 19 – 20: The Lord looked down from his sanctuary on high, from Heaven he viewed the earth, to hear the groans of the prisoners and release those condemned to death.*

L ord, I have felt the chains with every move, and they cried out in a never-ending mantra, "Condemned! condemned! condemned!" Born into a prison of sin and disobedience, I lived for the momentary cessation of the pain of living. I even took pride in my sinful actions, as if I were a stronger man, or more of a man, because I could bear the weight of the chains of bondage. I had already been judged unworthy of any fate but that of eternal damnation, a soul in a miserable body waiting to be released to everlasting

Hell. But you, Lord, have cast off my chains, and they no longer cry out "condemned!" I have liberty and love, and the assurance of peace with you forever, oh Lord. You have changed my heritage and my inheritance.

Does your sin condemn you?
Romans 6:18, Romans 8:1, 1 John 1:19-20, John 3:17-18

JANUARY 23

Text: *Acts 3:19: Repent, then, and turn to God, so that your sins may be wiped out, that times of refreshing may come from the Lord.*

Repent! Why must we repent? Is it because we are afraid that if we do not that we won't go to heaven? Do we repent because someone we love wants us to repent? Do we repent because it is the thing to do in the church that we attend? Many of us repent for all the wrong reasons, and even hold the feeling, at times, that we are doing God a favor by repenting, rather like a drowning man feeling as if he is doing the lifeguard a favor by holding on to the life preserver that has been tossed to him. No! If we are to truly repent, we must understand that repentance is Jesus' gift to us! We are dying in our sin, and God reaches out His hand to save us from death and eternal damnation. We must repent because we are determined to accept His cleansing and then allow ourselves to receive his refreshing.

Why repent?
Jeremiah 15:19, Luke 15:10, Luke 13:4-5, Luke 5:31-32

JANUARY 24

Text: *Proverbs 23:23: Buy the truth and do not sell it; get wisdom, discipline and understanding.*

What is the price of truth, and where do we buy it? We buy truth from God, and it will cost us our pride, our ego, and the pleasure of fleshly sin. For truth will proclaim to us that our sin destroys us. Truth tells us that our sin will result in momentary pleasure and eternal damnation. It will cost us our denial that we love to dwell in. Where would we sell truth, and what price would we receive for it? We could sell it only at the shop of compromise, and it brings momentary satisfaction. It brings us acceptance by others who sin, an ersatz peace of mind in deception, in denial. But no matter how often we sell truth, it is ever before us. Whether it is ours, or we have sold it, it is ever-present in our lives.

How much is the truth worth to you?
Romans 1:23-25, Matthew 13:44, John 8:31-32, Psalm 145:18

JANUARY 25

Text: *Proverbs 28:13: He who conceals his sins does not prosper, but whoever confesses and renounces them finds mercy.*

The overt sins are more readily accessible. They are easy to find, although often times hard to let go. But there are deeper sins, which I often don't even think of as sin, I simply live in their comfort. I am rebuffed in some way by a loved one, and without good reason I feel rejected. The rejection leads me back to the sins that I think I have overcome. I say to myself, "I don't need you; I don't need anyone," and I crawl into my hiding place of self, all alone, to pout. I won't even let God into this place. That, of course, is the underlying sin, the more grievous sin, and the sin that cries out for confession. And so, I confess it and renounce it. I do need others, especially my Lord Jesus. I cannot hide from His love and mercy.

Do you hide from God?

Jeremiah 16:17, Hebrews 4:13, Jeremiah 23:24, Psalm 139:7

JANUARY 26

Text: *Luke 5:23: Which is easier: to say, "Your sins are forgiven," or to say, "Get up and walk?"*

The world, when it sees someone healed, celebrates and believes because people see the healing with their eyes. But just as in Jesus' time, it is much harder to believe that our Lord has forgiven sin. After all, we have sinned, and we deserve to be miserable and suffer for our sin. If Jesus heals us, is He going to take away the punishment that we so richly deserve? There are many in the world who will say, "That's not fair, you deserve what you get because you have sinned." But wasn't the torture that Jesus endured on the cross enough punishment for our sin? If Jesus forgives us, doesn't He substitute His punishment for ours? We speak not of natural consequences of sin, for those must be dealt with as Jesus allows. But Jesus can forgive our sin, and He will if we abandon our sin and ask Him for forgiveness.

Has God forgiven you?

Luke 23:34, 1 John 1:8-9, Ephesians 1:7-8, Isaiah 1:18

JANUARY 27

Text: *Luke 13:27: But he will answer, "I don't know you or where you come from. Away from me, all you evildoers."*

These are the most horrible words in eternity, spoken by God at the moment we kneel before Him. He will say to some, even to some who have made a profession of faith, "I don't know you, for the evil that you have done clothes you, and I cannot recognize the child beneath the evil." It is not enough for me to say that I believe in Jesus. If I say that I believe in the principles of aerodynamics but refuse to take off in an airplane, my actions cover my words of belief and affirmation, and all that the world knows is that I refuse to fly. Only God knows my heart. I must, we must, repent of the evil that we do and confess it so that it is gone from our souls when we stand before God.

Is there evil in your heart?
Psalm 51:10-11, Psalm 139:23-24, Romans 1:21, 2 Corinthians 5:10

JANUARY 28

Text: *Luke 18:41: What do you want me to do for you?*

These are the words of Jesus to a blind beggar sitting on the side of the road, calling out for God's mercy. Why did Jesus even ask the question? I believe that he asked so that the blind man would confront the truth. I have prayed for many things, for healing of sin, for so long that I have become accustomed to praying and have abandoned hope of my prayers being answered. I have learned to accommodate. I have become, if not comfortable, at least used to my situation, and so my prayers have become professions of acceptance of my situation, and I really do not expect healing. Perhaps I really

19

don't want my situation to change, for if it changes I will have to be responsible for living a healed life. The question for me, and for you, is really, "What do we want Jesus to do for us?"

Do you really want to be healed?
Revelation 3:21, 1 John 5:3-4, Philippians 1:6, 2 Chronicles 15:7

JANUARY 29

Text: Psalm 51:2: Wash away all my iniquity and cleanse me from my sin.

Sometimes I come before my Lord with the plea that He will wash away some of my iniquity, or even most of my iniquity. I must admit that often when I would admit my sin, I didn't want Him to take away all my sin. I wanted to keep a portion, because it brought pleasure to my flesh. I am like the man who bathes and dresses in new clothing but neglects to shine his shoes. No one will really notice the new clothes, but they will all notice his shoes. No! When I confess before my Lord, I must really want to be cleansed of ALL my sin. I must not hold any sin back. I cannot stash away any temptation for future use. I must give it all to my Lord, and truly confess, that I may really be cleansed.

Do you hide some sin from God?
Proverbs 28:13, Psalm 32:3-5, Isaiah 29:15, 2 Kings 17:9

JANUARY 30

Text: *Psalm 51:4: Against you, you only, have I sinned and done evil in your sight.*

When I have sinned, my sin has hurt God's people, the people that He loves. To the best of my ability, I have made right what I did to harm them. But my real sin was against the Lord. After He died to cleanse me of my sin, and with full knowledge of His suffering on the cross to save me, I deliberately went out again and did things directly in violation of God's law. I know how my sin hurts the Lord. Help me, Oh Lord, to think about what I am doing with every temptation that is put before me, and help me to choose you, Lord, rather than the sin. For in the end, Lord, I stand before you and you alone, and I will be accountable to you.

Against whom do you sin?
Psalm 78:40-41, Hebrews 10:29, 1 Peter 2:24, Isaiah 53:5

JANUARY 31

Text: *Psalm 90:8: You have set our iniquities before you, our secret sins in the light of your presence.*

I have learned from a young age (and the world has taught me) how to hide my real self from everyone. Since the world does not find my sin to be acceptable, I simply take steps to keep the world from knowing. Especially do I hide from my loved ones. I have this need to appear clean in their eyes, and my pride dictates that I appear to be a sinless, God-fearing man. But you know, oh Lord, all my sin; it is ever before you. What I have kept secret from the world, I cannot keep secret from you. All of my sin is arrayed before you, and you hate my sin, but you love me, Lord. Let me walk into your light now, and examine me in my sin, that I may be forgiven.

Have you hidden yourself from the world?
2 Timothy 3:5, 1 Samuel 16:7, Proverbs 28:13, Matthew 23:27-28

FEBRUARY

FEBRUARY 1

Text: *Psalm 119:5: Oh that my ways were steadfast in obeying your decrees!*

Lord you have set forth your law by decree. You have come to man and held out the royal scepter in a high place and announced in a mighty voice that all might hear that your law is as you set forth, as you decreed. None may claim ignorance of your mighty decree. Oh Lord, that I were obedient, but I am not. In small sin, I trespass against your law. In horrendous evil, I flaunt my abandon of the very words you have spoken to me. I confess, Lord, that I have sinned before you and have thrown my sin in your face. But, Lord, I have repented of my rebellion, and I desire to be steadfast in the keeping of your law. Help me now to turn from my sin to your holy way.

> *Do you accept "small" sin in your life?*
> *Matthew 5:17-18, 1 John 3:4, 1 John 5:17, James 2:10*

FEBRUARY 2

Text: *Psalm 120:2: Deliver my soul, O Lord, from lying lips, from a deceitful tongue.*

Lord, my lips have learned to lie; my tongue has learned to be deceitful. My addiction, Lord, has taught me how to lie, for if I told the truth, I would be condemned and people would shun me. Those who loved me would love me no longer, and so I hid my disgrace in the lies. I lived with deceit and I hid in the labyrinth of falsehood. No one knew what I did. No one knew who I really was. But you knew Lord, the whole time I was hiding from those who loved me, you knew, and you still know. I lied for so long it was hard to be truthful; but Lord, you dwell in truth. Deliver me Lord, from the lies that I have told, and cleanse my lips and make my voice a sweet sound of truth. As once I dwelt in falsehood, now, Lord, let me dwell in truth.

Are you afraid of the truth?
Psalm 27:1-3, Proverbs 28:13, 1 John 1:6, John 3:20

FEBRUARY 3

Text: *Psalm 122:9: For the sake of the house of the Lord our God, I will seek your good.*

I will seek your good, what is right and just, and honoring to you O Lord. For when my actions honor you, Lord, my brothers and sisters are honored as well. Your family is blessed; your house is increased. But, Lord, when I sin against your house, I dishonor and disgrace you first and foremost. And when I dishonor your house, my brothers and sisters are less because of my actions. I have often thought that since my sin is kept in secret, and hidden from the view of those in your house, that I have harmed no one but myself. I have been wrong. When I sin, you know, and all the angels and spirits in the heavenly places know, and your house is brought into disgrace, because I am your child.

What is the result of your sin?
Romans 14:15, Isaiah 59:2, Colossians 3:5-6, Galatians 6:7-8

FEBRUARY 4

Text: *Proverbs 30:20: This is the way of an adulteress: She eats and wipes her mouth and says "I've done nothing wrong."*

It is the way of a sinner whose conscience has been seared. When first I fell into sin I was appalled at my own actions; I couldn't believe what I had done. The second time was easier, and the third time bothered me even less, as I was tempted by ever greater sin and greater evil. One day I looked back and laughed at my consternation over the first sin and told myself that my unnatural way of living was really natural for, after all, I was only human and thus doomed to fail. And so, I wiped my mouth, and said I have done nothing wrong, even though I knew it was a lie. I must return to the horror and shame of that first sin, to the understanding of the tragedy that it was. My repentance must begin there.

Do you take your sin seriously?

1 John 3:4, Hebrews 10:26-27, Deuteronomy 30:17-18, James 1: 14-15

FEBRUARY 5

Text: *Psalms 51:17: The sacrifices of God are a broken spirit; a broken and contrite heart, O God, you will not despise.*

What can I offer you, O Lord, for all that I possess belongs to you. I can give you my time and my hard work, but unless it flows from a relationship with you it is meaningless. What I must bring to you is my total love and adoration, and I must receive your love for me. I cannot offer my life to you unless we share a relationship forged of experience. I must experience the same broken spirit and broken heart that you experience when I have sinned against you. Father let those sins and times of sin lead my heart to contrition and let my guilt break my spirit, the spirit of "me," before your altar. This sacrifice I offer to you.

What will you sacrifice to God today?

Hebrews 13:15-16, Romans 12:1, 1 Samuel 15:22, Psalm 51: 16-17

FEBRUARY 6

Text: *Acts 19:18: Many of those who believed now came and openly confessed their evil deeds.*

Men, using the power of God, but not living for God, had just been exposed. Through this example God spoke to Christians, living in fellowship with other Christians, but also living with hidden sin in their lives. Suddenly they were shown a great lesson. Some who used the name of Jesus, but knew Him not, were trying to use Jesus for their own purposes, pretending to be Christians when they were not. For the Christians who saw this, it was a wake-up call. They needed to repent of the sin in their lives so that they might have nothing hidden from God or their fellow believers. They now knew that God was serious about their lives and that they could no longer live a life divided between God and sin. God teaches me the same lesson today. I must, out of fear, or respect for God, openly confess my sin to God and to my fellow believers.

> *Will you admit your sin to your brothers and sisters?*
> *James 5:16, Proverbs 28:13, John 20:21-22, Ephesians 5:11*

FEBRUARY 7

Text: *Revelation 17:1 &2: Come here, I shall show you the judgment of the great harlot who sits on many waters, with whom the kings of the earth committed acts of immorality and those who dwell on the earth were made drunk with the wine of her immorality.*

The great harlot is "the city" which reigns over the Earth. A real city? Perhaps. A figure of speech or a symbol of that which draws people away from a simple life and walk with God and into the pursuit of wealth and power? Both? Only God knows, but his word tells us something much more important. Man's mind wants to solve the mystery of *who*, when the important lesson is *what*, and God points that out very clearly. The passage speaks of abominations, sexual sin, ritual killing, and filthy, terrible sin. But the sin is not the cause for God's judgment. It is the product of relationship with the enemy, the beast. No, the real cause for the judgment upon man is that man has turned from relationship with God to a relationship with the fallen angel of God, and disobedience. True repentance deals with relationship.

Who do you walk with?

2 Corinthians 6:14-16, Psalm 1:1, Proverbs 4:18-19, 1 Corinthians 15:33

FEBRUARY 8

Text: *Psalm 25:11: For the sake of your name O Lord, forgive my iniquity, though it is great.*

Lord, I am not worthy even to ask that you forgive my sin for I have sinned deliberately. It was not a mistake or an accident that I sinned. It was not something that the enemy thrust upon me, although he certainly led me and provided abundant opportunity. No Lord, I cannot blame anyone else, not even Satan himself, for my deliberate actions, for the choices that I have made. For I have made the choices willingly, knowingly, and deliberately. My sin, Lord, has been against you. But even as unworthy as I am to receive your forgiveness, you have spoken to me of your great love for me, and have promised that as I come to you, you will restore me. Lord, because you have promised in your name, I am forgiven.

Is your sin deliberate?

Hebrews 10:26-27, 2 Timothy 2:13, Luke 12:47-48, Psalm 19:13

FEBRUARY 9

Text: *Psalm 36:5: Your love, O Lord, reaches to the heavens, your faithfulness to the skies.*

Lord these are the words I need to hear today. I have been tempted and have given in to the temptation. I didn't go far in my sin before I stopped, but your word doesn't describe or excuse "small sins." And now, this morning, even this morning, you tell me that your love for me reaches to the heavens, because I have confessed and repented of my sin. It is so great that it fills me and fills the Earth and overflows even into the heavens. Even though I have not been faithful to you, Father, you are faithful to me. Your faithfulness surrounds me and blesses me and leads me back into relationship with you. Lord, you are faithful in your love for me. Help me now to be faithful to you.

> *Do you find joy in repentance and forgiveness?*
> *Psalm 30:11, Luke 15:7, Acts 3:19, Psalm 32:1-2*

FEBRUARY 10

Text: *Psalm 109:6: Appoint a wicked man over him; and let an accuser stand at his right hand.*

And so David recalls his righteous anger toward Saul and the people who had turned against him. He rails against injustice, treachery, and betrayal. He asks God to send evil upon Saul and the people who follow him. His anger is righteous. Saul really did have it coming to him. He was evil and demented and deserved God's judgment. Would David have a righteous anger against me today? Does God have a righteous anger against me? Have I taken in sin and abused that which was given to me in God's love? Have my actions caused the innocent to sin alongside of me? In order for me to avoid God's righteous anger, I must come to him humbly and truly repent, for He has every right to be angry.

Is God angry with you or with your sin?
Romans 1:18, Isaiah 59:2, Ephesians 5:6, Psalm 30:5

FEBRUARY 11

Text: *Romans 6:5: If we have been united with him like this in his death, we will certainly also be united with him in his resurrection.*

As Jesus hung on the cross and died a horrendous death, I know that my sin was there. But sometimes—no--most of the time, I view the scene as a spectator. I am an observer, leaving my sin at the cross and watching Jesus die for me, and I am wrong. I must not, I cannot, stand and watch, but rather I must climb the hill, place myself on the cross and die with Jesus on that cross. Yes, of course, it is a painful death. Leaving the sinful life I have led to give it all up on the cross is not supposed to be easy. It wasn't easy for Jesus to die; it isn't easy for me. It is necessary. I must surrender to this death.

Are you willing to die with Jesus?
2 Corinthians 5:14-15, Galatians 2:20, Luke 9:24, Romans 6:6

FEBRUARY 12

Text: *Psalm 118:8: It is better to take refuge in the Lord than to trust in man.*

I struggled against temptation every day. I read many books about my addiction; I went to see counselors and therapists. I joined groups, and became part of studies. But always I returned to the addiction. It was a force in my life that I was unable to control. It was my default position when I needed to be comforted, excited, or when I simply desired to find pleasure. I began to look at my addiction, and my attempts to overcome it, with resignation, and said to myself, "That's just who I am; I can't change." I was right, I could not change, but God changed me, by showing me that this was not who I was; that I was created in His image to stand pure and holy before Him. He showed me that He would do for me what I could not do for myself. Now I must continue to work to preserve the gift that He has given to me, but all the while I must trust Him, not me.

Do you trust the world for healing?
Proverbs 28:26, Psalm 91:1-2, John 3:16, Ephesians 1:7-8

FEBRUARY 13

Text: *Proverbs 23:26: My son, give me your heart, and let your eyes keep to my ways.*

We must not let our eyes be distracted by hearts that seek after the world. The very God of creation, the Lord that knit us together in our mothers' wombs, who placed our hearts in our chests and commanded them to beat, when he calls us to give him those hearts, our hearts, he does not want just a part of our heart, but all of it. I have cried out to God, "What do you want of me, Lord; I am only a man and can only give so much." But God replied to me, "No. I have created you and I know that you can give me your all, and that's what I demand." My eyes have betrayed me like the eyes of a child in a toy store, darting here and darting there, tempted by all the bright colors and displays of the world. I must not let the world distract me. I must focus on the word, not the world. I must be attentive to His ways, and only then will I be able to give all to the Lord. I must surrender all.

What in the world are you looking at?

Hebrews 12:1-2, Proverbs 27:20, Psalm 119:37, 1 John 2:15-16

FEBRUARY 14

Text: *Luke 12:48: From everyone who has been given much, much will be demanded.*

What has God given to you? What has He given to me? With what have we been entrusted: wealth, power, position, or riches? They are all irrelevant; they matter not to God. He has given us our salvation. He has given us death to sin with His death on the cross, and power in the heavenly places as we are resurrected with him. He has given us freedom from the sin that held us so tightly in bondage to our flesh and to Satan. So, what now is asked of us? What now is required? Jesus asks only for my life, and my heart and my soul--all of it. Not a mite can I withhold. Jesus gave all of that, and more, for me, and now requires that of me. I must fulfill my obligation. I have incurred a great debt, and I must pay in the freedom that God gives to me.

What will you do with God's gift?
1 Peter 4:10, Matthew 55:14-16, Philippians 2:4-5, Matthew 10:8

FEBRUARY 15

Text: *Deuteronomy 30: 15, 19: See, I set before you today life and prosperity, death and destruction. v. 19 ...now choose life....*

Lord I have gone through a time in which I have been disobedient to you. I am often reminded of my times of disobedience. Now Lord, you come to me, in your word, and make it so simple that not even I can over-complicate it. I must choose, once and for all, life or death. I must choose blessings or curses. I must choose between the world of the Holy Spirit and this world. I must choose between you and Satan. I must choose between my flesh and my soul. I choose you, Lord. Now I pray that you will keep me strong in my resolve, consistent in my obedience, and close in my walk with you. Today, Lord, I choose life. Today, Lord, I choose you.

What do you choose today?

Psalm 119:30 Joshua 24:15, Matthew 7:13-14, 1 Kings 18:21

FEBRUARY 16

Text: *Deuteronomy 32:12: The Lord alone led him; no foreign god was with him.*

Lord, may you alone lead me. Let there be no foreign gods that I follow. In order, Lord, for you to lead me, I must be willing to follow. But Lord, you lead me on hard paths. The other gods have led me down fun paths, easy paths, paths that titillate the flesh and exalt me instead of you. But, Lord, I have seen the end of those paths and I have stared at the fires of Hell that wait to consume my flesh and my soul. I reject those paths no matter how pleasant they might appear. Your paths, Lord, are often hard and take me to places that are difficult. The climb into the high places is often exhausting and my body cries out from fatigue. But you have shown me the high places, the Promised Land at the end of your path. It is the place where we will dwell together for eternity, and so I forsake all others for you.

What path have you chosen?

Psalm 119:101-105, Proverbs 3:6, Hebrews 12:12-13, Proverbs 4:18-19

FEBRUARY 17

Text: *Ezra 3: 6: On the first day of the third month they began to offer burnt offerings to the Lord, though the foundation of the Lord's temple had not yet been laid.*

God's chosen people have returned to Jerusalem to rebuild the temple, the city, and their lives after the years of Babylonian captivity. Their specific job, one of the terms of their release, was to see that the temple was rebuilt. They finally got it right. Before the foundation of the temple was laid, before the construction of the temple, before they rebuilt their city, they offered sacrifice to the Lord and sang in praise of God. Even so today, Lord, let me finally get it right. In my life I have been taken captive by the Holy Spirit's enemy who rules this world, and by my own sin nature. The enemy did not let me go, but God plucked me from the modern-day Babylon of a sinful world. As I begin to rebuild my life, let me first, before I do anything else, honor God and give Him praise.

Is praise your daily priority?
1 Chronicles 16:24-25, 2 Kings 17:39, Hebrews 13:15, Psalm 100:1-5

FEBRUARY 18

Text: *Job 19: 4: If it is true that I have gone astray, my error remains my concern alone.*

Job cries out in his pain and desolation and says to the world: "If I have sin in my life it's between me and God; it's none of your business." Sin, by its very nature, tempts us to feel that way. I, too, in my sin felt that and, as long as I did and believed the lie of the enemy, my sin remained hidden and grew like a fire in a closet within me. But, when I tore down the door to the hiding place of my sin, and exposed my sin to the light, the fire was dampened and the fuel it found in darkness was then removed. Thank you, Lord.

Are you hiding your sin?
Proverbs 28:13, Isaiah 29:15, Ephesians 5:8-14, John 3:19-21

FEBRUARY 19

Text: *Ezekiel 46:15: So the lamb and the grain offering and the oil shall be provided morning by morning for a regular burnt offering.*

Lord, it was your command to your people that they were to provide the sacrifice to you on a daily basis. That's a lot of sacrifice. But Lord, if you command your people to do something, you will provide them with the means to do it. You provided the lambs and the grain and the oil, and your people were blessed because they too always had enough. Lord, today, even today, you provide whatever is needed to keep your commands. You will never give me a command without the resources necessary to obey your command. You have commanded me to abstain from sexual immorality and sexual sin. You will provide the strength and the ability to do so and the blessing that follows.

Where is your strength when tempted?
Philippians 4:13, 1 Corinthians 10:13, Psalm 121:1-3, James 4:7-10

FEBRUARY 20

Text: *Proverbs 15:22: Plans fail for lack of counsel, but with many advisors they succeed.*

Trapped in sin and seeking the Lord, I wanted desperately to find purity, and to walk free of the mire that had trapped me. But as I sought God and sought to be whole, another sin subtly took up residence in my thoughts. It was the root of pride that is born in every man. The pride told me that I could do it alone. I not only did not need anyone else, but if I ever really honestly told anyone else about my sin, they would surely reject me. What would they think, and how would they react? I decided not to confide in anyone else; it would be enough that I admitted my sin to God. But God's word tells us to set aside our pride, and fear, and choose carefully a brother who will love us, and then enlist his counsel so that there will be a true brother to hold us accountable to God's commands.

Will you admit your sin?
Proverbs 29:25, James 5:16, 1 John 1:9, Psalm 32:3

FEBRUARY 21

Text: *Psalms 119:112: My heart is set on keeping your decrees to the very end.*

Lord, I know not what lies ahead, but you have made me to know that we are about to embark on an adventure; that I am to have no fear; that it will be exciting and difficult; but that it will be our adventure and you will partner with me. And so, Lord, help me to keep your decrees throughout the adventure. You are the senior partner; you head up the operation, and I will keep your decrees and listen for your voice as we start out. I don't know where we're going Lord, you and I, but when your voice says go, I will go. When you tell me to stop and rest, I will rest. When you tell me to speak, I will speak your words that you give to me. I will trust you to lead me and I will obey. I am excited, Lord, as you show me how to prepare for this trip.

Who will lead your journey?
Mark 8:34, John 12:26, Jeremiah 29:11, Psalm 1:1-3

FEBRUARY 22

Text: *Luke 18:34: The disciples did not understand any of this. Its meaning was hidden from them, and they did not know what he was talking about.*

The disciples expected triumph. They believed and had faith in Jesus as the conquering king, the Son of God, whose reign on the Earth was about to begin. In fact, they were right, but they did not expect, nor could they understand, that it would come through death and resurrection. God spoke clearly but the disciples listened with ears plugged with expectations that were not God's way. When I pray for deliverance from my besetting sins, I pray for instant deliverance, an immediate cessation of all temptation. Although that is possible--for nothing is impossible for God--it is usually not the way that God answers. I must be prepared to hear of a long hard battle to kill the sin that I have allowed in my flesh, and for resurrection only in obedience to God's command. I want to hear about the easy way, but Lord, help me to hear the truth.

Will you endure the struggle to be free?
Hebrews 12:3-4, 1 Peter 4:12-13, James 1:2-4, Matthew 24:13

FEBRUARY 23

Text: *Luke 20:18: Everyone who falls on that stone will be broken to pieces, but he on whom it falls will be crushed.*

The stone is confession. The stone is repentance. The stone is true sorrow for having sinned. The stone is Jesus. If I would be saved out of my lust and addiction to the demands of my flesh, I must be broken into pieces. As long as I think that I am whole, I will rely on my own strength. I will say things like, "I can stop doing this," or "What I'm doing isn't really so bad," or "Everybody does this kind of thing, surely God doesn't care." But, the lies are the cement of a false god of self-sufficiency. I must not hesitate to fall on the rock to be broken, for as I do, I will be made truly whole. But should I fail and refuse the rock, it will come to me, and at the moment of my greatest strength I will be crushed.

Will you be broken?

Psalm 51:17, Matthew 5:3, Psalm 147:3, Jeremiah 18:3-4

FEBRUARY 24

Text: *Revelation 2:10: Do not be afraid of what you are about to suffer.*

How can I be about to suffer and not be afraid? Did not even our Lord Jesus, in his flesh, fear what he was about to suffer when he was in Gethsemane? Perhaps I know what I am about to suffer, and I tremble. Perhaps I don't know what I will suffer and that is just as bad, if not worse. I fear the "what ifs." I see my life and the impending storms, and I say to myself, "What if this happens?" or "What if that happens?" and then I imagine the worst-case scenario. Jesus in the garden did not imagine: Jesus knew. It was the worst-case scenario, and his flesh trembled, but he was confident in his Father. In the spirit He knew that even in the midst of trial, his Father would watch over Him. Even though my flesh cries out in fear, I too can trust God in His spirit, and of course this is what the word means when God says to us, "Do not be afraid."

What do you do with the "what ifs"?
Matthew 6:31-34, Psalm 91:1-16, Philippians 4:6-7, Psalm 23:4

FEBRUARY 25

Text: *Psalm 42:11: Why are you downcast O my soul? Why so disturbed within me? Put your hope in God for I will yet praise him, my savior and my God.*

My soul is downcast because once again the enemy has been knocking at my door seeking entry to my heart of hearts, that he might fill my life with lies. When the door is opened just a crack, the first lie that he pushes in is guilt and shame. Lord, Satan is telling me that I am not really your child, and that I will never be able to stop his lies to me and my surrender to temptation. Since it is from Satan, (and I am convinced that it is, because your voice tells me that you love me) then it must be a lie, and I reject Satan's lies. Lord, you are mine and I belong to you. Take my soul, O Lord, and satisfy me with your presence. I am in love with only you, and I will yet praise you.

Whose child are you?
1 John 3:1-3, John 1:12-13, Romans 8:16, 2 Corinthians 6:18

FEBRUARY 26

Text: *Psalm 84:12: O Lord almighty, blessed is the man who trusts in you.*

Lord, as we walk through our lives, each one of us, you have not promised that it would be easy, and it is not. You did not say to us that you would shower riches down upon us, and surely we have had to work all our days to prosper. You did not tell us that we would not see wars and famine, and despots and death, for we have seen far too much of these things. But Lord you did tell us that if our faith does not stagger, if we continue to believe in you and to trust you in what you will do, and in all that we do and see and suffer, that we will be blessed. We will be blessed not by our circumstances but because we can trust you in every circumstance.

Do you trust God in every circumstance?
Psalm 56:3-4, Proverbs 3:5-6, 1 John 5:14-15, Psalm 9:10

FEBRUARY 27

Text: *Psalm 18:46: The Lord lives! Praise be to my Rock! Exalted be God my Savior!*

I serve not A living god, but I serve THE living God. All other gods are either carved from stone or wood, or exist only in the minds of mortals or are mortals themselves. They are not even to be considered minor gods, for they are not gods at all. Only God is God, and He will not only live forever, He has always lived forever, and best of all, for me, is that He lives today in me. He is my rock; the never-changing foundation of my being that cannot and will not be shaken. Sometimes there are storms and waves that batter the rock on which I stand, and sometimes I am in danger of being swept away by the raging waters. But the rock raises clefts to hide me, and the rock is never moved. I praise you, O God, for finding me and saving me, for being my God and being immovable.

Is God your rock?

Psalm 78:35, 2 Samuel 22:32, Psalm 92:15, Psalm 84:26

FEBRUARY 28

Text: *Psalm 31: 14 & 15: But as for me I trust in thee, O Lord; I say, "You are my God." My times are in your hands; deliver me from my enemies and from those who pursue me.*

Lord, I am persecuted by temptation, and my enemies are the minions of Satan and even Satan himself. But you, O Lord, will deliver me from my enemies, from all of my enemies and from the persecution of temptation to sin. I don't know, nor can I understand how others deal with their enemies. I don't even know, nor should I, what or who their enemies are. All I know, O Lord, is what I face each day--and I choose you. I put all my trust in you. I do not reserve any trust in case you fail me, for I know that you will never fail me. I put no trust in anything or anyone else or in myself, because I have known nothing but failure from others and from my own efforts. You are my God.

Who is your enemy?

Ephesians 6:12, 1 Peter 5:8-9, 2 Corinthians 10:3-5, 1 John 4:2-3

FEBRUARY 29

Text: *John 4:50: Jesus replied, "You may go. Your son will live." The man took Jesus at his word and departed.*

Do I have as much faith and courage as this man? Did He really have faith? If it had been me, I might have just given up. I might have believed that Jesus was just placating me, and that He wasn't going to do anything to help me anyway. In fact, I have often felt that way about the disease of sexual sin that rages in my body. But the word says that the man took Jesus at his word. He believed Jesus and returned to his son. I believe that a reason for his faith was that he was actually in the presence of Jesus. I, too, can have this kind of faith, because Jesus is still here, and I am in His presence. Let me take Jesus at His word.

Do you believe what Jesus tells you?
Mark 9:22-24, John 20:27, Hebrews 11:1, John 11:40

MARCH

MARCH 1

Text: *Judges 7:3: ...anyone who trembles with fear may turn back....*

Lord, first you weaned out those who were afraid. Why were they afraid? Why did they tremble with fear? Perhaps, Lord, they didn't really understand what was going on. Perhaps they had not heard your voice, assuring them of victory, because they had not taken the time to listen. Perhaps they had heard your voice, but still had doubts. Their faith in you was not strong enough to sustain them in battle. Lord, in my battles, I sometimes tremble and am often afraid, but I am in the fight. You have equipped me; you have filled my quiver with arrows and cemented my hand to the sword. Lord, I will go forth in the battle even unto death if that is your plan. My faith is in you and in your mighty hand. Increase my faith.

> *Do you have enough faith for the fight?*
> *1 Corinthians 16:13, Galatians 2:20, Isaiah 41:10, 1 Timothy 6:12*

MARCH 2

Text: *Judges 5:21: March on my soul, be strong.*

These are the words of Deborah after the victory she shared with Barak, and yet, it was not their victory, Lord, it was yours. Just as you called your people to be warriors in the days of the judges, you have called me, today, to be a warrior. The Old Testament speaks of enemies of flesh and blood, kingdoms and arms. My enemy is the nameless, faceless evil of Hell. It would be easier, perhaps, for me to go to war against man than to go to war against this enemy. But, Lord, you have known from the beginning of time the enemy that you called me to fight--and fight I will. I don't need chariots, or spears, or men on horses, nor do I need archers. Lord, all that I need you have provided: the inner strength, the power of your Holy Spirit, your Word, and prayer. I am clad in your armor and in the midst of battle even now. March on my soul--be strong.

Where do you get your power?

Acts 1:8, Isaiah 40:31, Psalm 28:7-8, 2 Corinthians 12:9

MARCH 3

Text: *Mark 10:48: Many rebuked him and told him to be quiet, but he shouted all the more, "Son of David, have mercy on me."*

Lord, we must all be blind Bartimaeus, for we are all blind--especially me. I am blinded by sin and temptation, ego and knowledge, comfort and wealth. I need to sit by the side of the road and call out to you in the midst of the crowd, not caring that others think me a fool. I must be so desperate for healing that I am willing to be foolish before the world, willing to endure the ridicule of the world, and the taunting of the unbeliever. Only then will I have enough faith for you to turn and say, "Your faith has healed you."

Will you be foolish for God?

1 Corinthians 1:27, 1 Corinthians 4:9-10, Luke 9:25-26, 1 Peter 4:13-14

MARCH 4

Text: *1 Samuel 17:26: Who is this uncircumcised Philistine that he should defy the armies of the living God?*

Goliath, for forty days, had been spitting in the face of God's people. He had held them captive to fear, and stripped them of any strength they possessed, because they were afraid to use the strength they had been given. He had caused them to forget that they were the sons of the living

God. Sin is the Goliath of many lives today: it is my Goliath. It yells at me, screams, and spits in my face. I see the enormity of the attraction that the flesh has for sin, and I am afraid. I cower in my armor, as my spirit is insulted by sin. But still, today, I will follow David and say, "What is this flesh that it should defy the power of the Holy Spirit that lives in me?" I must, and I will, kill the evil and the fear.

> *What are you afraid of?*
> *Psalm 34:4, Psalm 91:5-6, Matthew 10:28, John 14:27*

MARCH 5

Text: *Revelation 1:7: Look, he is coming with the clouds, and every eye will see him, even those who pierced him.*

Jesus, my Lord, is coming back. It is easy for me to understand intellectually that when Jesus suffered on the cross, he suffered because of my sins. He suffered because I betrayed him. But when Jesus returns, I will gaze into his eyes and, for the first time, I will know on a different level than I now know the pain and suffering I caused. It will be the difference between the soldier who knows that his rifle fire has killed another, and the soldier who shoots someone and watches the person die before his eyes. I will experience the grief that my sin has caused in Jesus. But Jesus says those sins will be gone, and when He comes again, not only will they be gone for Him, but I will finally be able to lay them aside. I will know that He has cleansed me.

> *Is your sin at the cross?*
> *1 Peter 2:24, Isaiah 53:5, Romans 6:6-7, 1 Peter 3:18*

MARCH 6

Text: *2 Kings 21:7: He took the carved Asherah pole he had made and put it in the temple.*

Manasseh followed the progression of sin that had been growing in his kingdom. It was the downward spiral that becomes darker and darker with each succeeding generation of sin. His fathers had worshipped other gods, and they built temples to these other gods on the hillsides, and even placed Asherahs in the holy temple that Solomon had built for God to abide in, the holy temple where God said He would dwell. But God's word tells me that when I asked Jesus into my life and heart, that my body became the temple of the Holy Spirit, and that God dwells in me. Do not I, also, build evil idols to foreign gods in God's temple? Only God can cleanse His temple, but I must ask to be cleansed.

Are there false idols in your temple?
1 Corinthians 3:16-17, 1 Peter 2:5, 1 Corinthians 10:14, Exodus 20:2-3

MARCH 7

Text: *Psalm 119:101: I have kept my feet from every evil path so that I might obey your word.*

I so desire that my life had been so, but it was not. I have trod the evil paths, even frolicked on them, and I did so willingly. I look back at the places where I have been with such great regret and sorrow, and I look forward and see new paths that will tempt me, and I am afraid. I have covered my life with remorse and shame, but God has said to me that my sin is gone, and with it, my shame has fled. God has forgotten my sin, but I dare not forget, for if I were to forget I would be doomed to repeat my sin, and I could not reach out to others who are still caught up in the evil. God tells me to look forward with joy, for He will lead me into His paths, and I will be cleansed.

What path will you walk?

Hebrews 12:13, Proverbs 4:14-15, Matthew 7:13-14, Psalm 119:1-3

MARCH 8

Text: *Mark 15:24: And they crucified Him, and divided up his garments among themselves, casting lots for them, to decide what each should take.*

Before his life ended, Jesus was stripped naked. It was an act designed to humiliate Him and leave Him hanging on the cross, naked and exposed, for all to see. But it was more. Jesus died as He was born and as He lived, discarding anything of the Earth, and ascending to the Father cleansed of all impurity. Jesus was stripped of all the things of this world in order to be prepared to enter the next. When Jesus reappeared, He was clad in heavenly robes, His old clothing was simply not appropriate for the resurrection. If I am to be "resurrected' from the cross of my sin, I, too, must be stripped of my sinful desires and fleshly lusts, to prepare me to walk with the resurrected Christ.

What must you discard?

Hebrews 12:1, Matthew 6:19-20, Colossians 3:1-3, Romans 12:2

MARCH 9

Text: *Job 23:10: But he knows the way that I take; when he has tested me, I will come forth as gold."*

God allows me to be tested, and I have been tested. Great impurity has been found in me. There is gold within my soul, but also much dross. But if the Lord did not allow the testing, how would I ever know where the impurity was, and what it was? And so, I ask my God to cleanse me of every impurity and help me to turn away and renounce the evil in my life, that after the testing, and after the purifying, I may be gold that is worthy of service to God.

> *Do you welcome God's testing?*
> *1 Peter 1:6-7, James 1:2-3, Psalm 66:10-12, Proverbs 17:3*

MARCH 10

Text: *Isaiah 1:18: Come now, let us reason together, says the Lord. Though your sins are like scarlet, they shall be as white as snow, though they are red as crimson, they shall be like wool.*

I thank my God, my savior, for healing me. The crimson of His blood has bleached the scarlet of my sins, so that I have become spotless in His eyes. Only the pure and holy God could do that for me. Only the love and power of the Holy Spirit would do that for me. Only the sacrifice of my friend Jesus on the cross did do that for me. I have been, I am, and I shall be cleansed pure white by the blood of God.

> *Has God's blood cleansed you?*
> *John 15:3, 1 John 1:9, 1 Corinthians 6:9-11, Ephesians 1:7*

MARCH 11

Text: *Exodus 39:1: They also made sacred garments for Aaron as the Lord commanded Moses.*

God's mercy is amazing. Moses traveled up the mountain where he was in the actual presence of God, and God gave to Moses the Ten Commandments. Meanwhile Aaron is down in the desert making a golden calf so that the people of God may worship a false god, directly in violation of God's first commandment. Yet, when Moses comes down the mountain, God instructs him on how, who, and where the people are to worship, and directs that Aaron will have the trappings of a priest and lead the people in worship. It is his mercy and his forgiveness, but it is also, I believe, that God will do whatever is necessary to accomplish His purposes. God's people were to worship Him. Aaron had led worship. God allowed Aaron to keep leading the worship in order that it would continue. He did not do this just for Aaron, but also for His people, that His will might be accomplished. He forgave Aaron in the process, as He forgives me. Perhaps I too may be a part of God's plan.

> *Has God called you to bless his people?*
> *2 Timothy 1:9, John 15:16, Proverbs 16:9, Jeremiah 29:11*

MARCH 12

Text: *Luke 17:4: If he sins against you seven times in a day, and seven times comes back to you and says "I repent," forgive him.*

This, of course, is instruction on how to deal with sin. As with all God's instruction, it is given that He might be revealed in us. This, then, is a picture of God's forgiveness that we are to model. I believe that what His word is saying to us is that we must continue to forgive as long as someone repents, just as He forgives us as we repent before Him. When I sin, I do hurt others, and I must repent and ask their forgiveness. But Lord, I have sinned against you, and I repent before you. Thank you, Lord, for your faithfulness to forgive.

Do you forgive as God forgives?
Ephesians 4:32, Matthew 6:14-15, Luke 6:37, Colossians 3:13

MARCH 13

Text: *Hebrews 9:22: In fact, the law requires that nearly everything be cleansed with blood, and without the shedding of blood there is no forgiveness.*

We are forgiven by the shedding of blood. It has always been so. In Old Testament days, the blood that was shed was of an animal, something owned by the person seeking forgiveness, something of value. It was an act of purchase. So it is now, only the price, the ultimate price, was paid by Jesus on the cross. He has purchased forgiveness for us with His own blood. It costs us nothing. It costs us everything. For unless we enter into a relationship with Jesus, unless we become one with Him, paying by giving up our all-- our desire for sin--we do not have the benefit of Jesus' ultimate sacrifice.

Are you willing to sacrifice?
Romans 12:1-2, Luke 9:23-25, Romans 6:13-14, Psalm 51:17

MARCH 14

Text: *Proverbs 20:22: Do not say "I'll pay you back for this wrong!" Wait for the Lord, and he will deliver you.*

So many of us with addictions in our life hang on to the wrongs that have been done to us. In some quarters, it is said that we are "just to get over it," and in others that we place the blame for our own sin on the actions of our parents or others, and we must "own our own sin." But the issue is not one of fault: it is an issue of forgiveness. If a person believes that he or she was mistreated, or not loved, or was rejected, it doesn't matter whether he was or not, because his belief is his reality. God says that if your belief has caused you to run to your addiction to bring salve to the wound, that you must release those who you believe have wronged you, so that God may deal with them, and that having forgiven them, that God may deal with you. We must come to the point at which there is the balm of Jesus, rather than the salve of temporary relief in sin.

> *What do you need to let go of?*
> *Proverbs 10:12, Isaiah 43:18-19, Philippians 3:13-14, Matthew 6:14*

MARCH 15

Text: *Psalm 25:18: Look upon my affliction and my distress and take away all my sins.*

Lord, I am afflicted, and I am distressed precisely because of my sins. I am haunted by the memories of that which I have done and that which I have failed to do. I am constantly aware of the presence of the enemy that awaits the opportunity to seize me when my flesh is weak. I can see the inevitable consequences of sin in my life. But you, O Lord, forgive my sins. Help me to accept your full and complete forgiveness, to see the consequences and go on. I must not dwell in what has happened. Help me to be more aware of the protection of your Holy Spirit than of the threats of the enemy. Take away from me the memories that accuse and condemn. Take away all my sin in your love and mercy. Forgive me completely.

Can you forget what God has forgiven?
2 Corinthians 5:17, Micah 7:19, Psalm 103:12, Romans 8:1

MARCH 16

Text: *Proverbs 21:31: The horse is made ready for the day of battle, but victory rests with the Lord.*

Victory is God's job. I must trust in His supreme power and authority and understand that He will be victorious in the battle against the enemy. But He has a job for me to do in the battle also, and I cannot ignore my responsibility by simply casting all responsibility on Him. If a soldier were to stay in bed all day, and never train, never learn how to fire a weapon, never work with the other members of his unit, do I think that he would remain a soldier? Even if he believed with all his heart that the battle belonged to the general and that his army would have ultimate victory, he would not be a soldier. In the same way I believe in Jesus' victory, but I must prepare, I must train for war, so that I will not be disqualified in the battle.

What is your part in the battle?
2 Chronicles 20:17, Ephesians 6:10-11, Psalm 144:1, Jeremiah 51:20-23

MARCH 17

Text: *Luke 15:10: In the same way, I tell you, there is joy in the presence of the angels of God over one sinner who repents.*

R ehab centers are not places of great social standing. People do not brag about visits to psychologists and counselors as they try to deal with sin and addiction. Sinners often repent and start the difficult journey to sobriety quietly. Recovery groups have anonymity as their hallmark. This is especially so with the sins of sexual addiction. Part of the addiction is the hiding and getting away with the sin--tricking the world so it does not know of the sin. Men sneak into porn shops and loiter at newsstands hoping their friends won't see them. Some men look for prostitutes in towns where no one knows them. Affairs are conducted in secret. But when a man repents, God and his angels proclaim it in joy, and all of heaven rejoices. Shouldn't we?

> *Do you hide your struggles?*
> *Proverbs 28:13, Psalm 32:3, James 5:16, Isaiah 24:15*

MARCH 18

Text: *Genesis 4:7: And if you do not do what is right, sin is crouching at your door; and it desires to have you, but you must master it.*

S in is ever crouching at my door when I do not "do well." When I take my eyes off of the Lord, when I start to slack off, when I start to compromise in the small things, Satan is waiting eagerly because he knows he can use the small flaws and chinks in the armor to start me on a path that leads to sin and devastation. I must keep my focus on God always, that I might not slip in little ways that lead to a fall. I do fear the sin that crouches at the door.

Help me Lord, to master that ever-present sin that would pounce upon my mistakes. It is my responsibility to keep your face ever before me.

Do you allow a "little sin" in your life?

James 1:15, Matthew 5:8, 1 Thessalonians 4:7, Ephesians 4:17-18

MARCH 19

Text: *2 Samuel 20:5: But when Amasa went to summon Judah, he took longer than the time the king had set for him.*

Even though he had been the commander of those who had fought against David, Amasa had been made the chief of all of David's warriors. But he blows the first assignment that King David gives him. In fact, he probably went back to the other side and was betraying King David. Joab, who was the warrior that David trusted during the years that he was besieged, is again placed in command of David's army. When Amasa meets him, Joab takes the opportunity to kill Amasa. Amasa had been honored by David, but along with the honor came responsibility, and David expected Amasa to work hard, fulfill his obligation, and certainly not to betray him. The Lord has honored me by giving me salvation and deliverance from besetting sin. He expects me to work hard at the tasks He has given me, to fulfill the law, and certainly not to betray Him by falling back into sin.

What does God expect of you?

Micah 6:8, 1 Peter 2:1-3, Isaiah 30:21-22, Ephesians 4:22-24

MARCH 20

Text: *Matthew 25:29: For everyone who has will be given more, and he will have an abundance. Whoever does not have, even what he has will be taken from him.*

Jesus gives us all a certain amount of faith, a certain amount of the gifting of God. It doesn't matter how much we are given; it matters what we do with it. The gifts are like muscles: the more they are used, the more they grow. Body builders are often times blessed genetically with great body structure, but if they never exercise their muscles, the muscles grow soft and flabby, and the person never reaches his or her potential. We are called upon to exercise our spiritual gifts, not only in our flight from sin, but also in giving glory to God. If we do not, even what we have been given will be taken from us.

Are you using God's gift?
1 Peter 4:10, 1 Timothy 4:14, James 1:17, 1 Corinthians 12:4-6

MARCH 21

Text: *Luke 6:49: But the one who hears my words and does not put them into practice is like a man who built a house on the ground without a foundation.*

What good is God's word to me if I ignore it? I am like a man who sets out on a journey of many miles and has a car with a full tank of gas and the keys in his pocket, but he decides to walk. The car is useless to him, and he will never reach his destination because he has made the decision not to use that which is his. I am so often that man. I hear God's word, I read God's word, but I do not use the word in my life. If I am to be whole, I must use God's word to me in order to heal. It is His word. It is my responsibility to use it.

What will you do with God's word?
Psalm 119:9, James 1:22-25, 2 Timothy 3:16-17, John 15:3-4

MARCH 22

Text: *John 5:6: Do you want to get well?*

A strange question to ask a man who has been lame for most, if not all, of his life? Not really. All the man knew how to do was to be crippled. He had been forced into the role of a beggar, a cripple, unable to walk, dependent on others to take care of him, and it was all he had ever known. If he were to be healed, he would quite literally have to stand on his own, support himself, and stop relying on others for help. Did he want to accept the responsibility for his own life that came from being healed? Do you? Do I? We are all crippled by sin. Do we really want to accept the responsibility of being healed, of being whole? Do you want to be healed? Do I?

> *Do you want to be healed?*
> *Galatians 6:5, Joshua 1:9, 2 Timothy 1:7, Psalm 55:22*

MARCH 23

Text: *Psalm 77:7: Will the Lord reject forever? Will he never show his face again?*

I have cried out to God in the midst of a sinful life. I have asked Him to deliver me, but God has been silent. Has the Lord rejected me? Have I lost God's blessing forever? Will I never again know the peace and comfort of His presence? But no! The Lord has told me that He has gone nowhere. He is still where I left Him, and I can return to God and to His open arms whenever I will. I turned away from Him and wandered off into a world of sin, and my loneliness and desolation caused me to cry out to Him, but I cried out for Him to come to me so I can have God without leaving my sin. God awaits my return. I cannot expect Him to come and dwell in the midst of my sin. It is my responsibility to turn from the sin and to Him, and He will pull me away from evil.

Will you leave your sin?
Psalm 119:59-61, Acts 3:19, Matthew 11:28, James 4:8

MARCH 24

Text: *1 Samuel 14:52: …and whenever Saul saw a mighty or any brave man, he took him into his service.*

It's called networking, and it's how the world works. Powerful people keep an eye out for the best, the smartest, the handsomest, and the richest. When they find them, they curry favor with them to make them an ally. They form power cliques and consolidate their power and stand against all that do not meet their standards. I have never been very good at this game. I don't think that I am considered valuable to most of those in power. They don't really want or need me. But then most of them don't really want or need Jesus either, because they don't believe that Jesus has anything to offer them. I must look around and see who I should cultivate, that I might not consolidate worldly power but rather multiply Holy Spirit power in this battle against the enemy and the sin that he brings upon me.

Do you seek worldly power or spiritual power?
Deuteronomy 8:17-18, 2 Corinthians 4:6-7, 1 John 4:4-6, 1 Corinthians 2:4-5

MARCH 25

Text: *Judges 1:2: The Lord answered. "Judah is to go; I have given the land into their hands."*

God called a specific people to a specific task at a specific time. He spoke to Judah, and they were to be the ones that were to conquer the Canaanites. God specifically gave a portion of the land into their hands. The men of Judah then called their brothers to the war with them, and the land of the Canaanites was given to them. I believe that even today the Lord calls men to Himself for a specific purpose, at a specific time, and that God intends for them to have a specific victory. I also believe it is God's will that we call upon our brothers to help us wage war against the enemy to achieve God's victory. We must see the land that we are to conquer. We must bring brothers alongside in the battle for our purity and our souls as we fight for our redemption.

> *For what has God called you?*
> *Romans 8:28, Proverbs 19:21, Psalm 32:8, Romans 11:29*

MARCH 26

Text: *1 Chronicles 19:13: Be strong, and let us show ourselves courageous for the sake of our people and for the cities of our God, and may the Lord do what is good in his sight.*

They were in battle. They were hemmed in by the enemy, and so they lined up back-to-back to take on their adversaries on all fronts. Even though surrounded, they left the outcome in the hand of God. What a great example for us as men facing the battle of sexual sin. We must come together as an army, line up, back-to-back, pledging to help each other in the battle and let the outcome of our struggle be in the hand of God. If I am to survive the battle, I must watch my brother's back and he must watch mine. We must be brave, and we must give the victory to God.

Where is your strength in battle?
2 Chronicles 20:15, Psalm 44:6-7, Joshua 1:9, Philippians 4:13

MARCH 27

Text: *Proverbs 17:17: A friend loves at all times, and a brother is born for adversity.*

If your friend does not love you when you have done something wrong, then he is not your friend. If you have a friend who is your brother, it is God's gift to you. This is the person who will stand with you in your temptation and your sin. When you are battling against the enemy, and the enemy is winning, and you are so ashamed, so down, so embarrassed that you can't speak to anyone about what you have done or what you are doing, he comes alongside and prays with you and for you. You don't even need to tell him the details; he will be there for you in any event. God has given, and will give, to each of us, brothers to confront, comfort, and strengthen us. We cannot overcome sin alone.

Who is your brother?
Proverbs 18:24, Romans 12:9-10, 1 John 3:16, Proverbs 27:17

MARCH 28

Text: *Psalm 142:7: Set me free from my prison, that I may praise your name. Then the righteous will gather about me because of your goodness to me.*

My soul has been imprisoned by my sinful addiction, and I cannot give thanks and glorify God's name for freeing me until I have been released. But even now, God is opening the prison gates and surrounding me with brothers who have stared at the same cell walls that imprison me. They will come alongside and show me what I must do. They will be my brothers. They will pray with me in the difficult times and rejoice in my triumphs as I walk again in the freedom of God's word and in His love. God has provided this band of brothers that I may be free to shout, to proclaim to the world that I am freed, and that I walk in righteousness before my God.

Are you imprisoned?

Romans 7:23, Galatians 3:22, 1 Peter 2:16, Psalm 107:14-15

MARCH 29

Text: *Proverbs 24:6: For waging war you need guidance, and for victory many advisers.*

Brothers, we are at war, and the stakes are high. No, nations will not crumble if we lose, but our world will fall apart. Just as a conquering army rape and pillages a country when it invades, so the enemy seeks to savage our souls. And, as the enemy occupies a land, Satan desires to camp in our lives and use us for his own purposes. If we are to fight, we need guidance. Programs, leaders, books, all provide the guidance. They direct us to the path that leads to victory; they are the battle plans that will defeat Satan's lascivious hordes. But one man standing against an army, even with a plan for battle, will surely fall. We must turn to advisors, those who have been in the fight and have struggled with this enemy, those who have been occupied but now are free. We must rely on their strength and experience to win this war. We must turn to the strength and experience of brothers.

Do you listen to counsel?

Proverbs 1:5, Proverbs 15:22, Hebrews 3:12-13, Colossians 3:16

MARCH 30

Text: *Acts 3:7: Taking him by the right hand, he helped him up, and instantly the man's feet became strong.*

The Apostles saw the infirmity and had sympathy for the crippled beggar. They spoke to him and pronounced healing. But the beggar was still unable to rise. The healing took place, miraculously and instantaneously, only after Peter bent down and lifted him to his feet. We may be crippled by our addictions, or we may have compassion for someone who has been crippled by his addiction. It is of no use to say "I heal you" unless God chooses to act sovereignly. How many times have we, as addicts, renounced our sin, sworn not to sin again, and trusted on the Lord's strength to keep us from sin, yet we have gone back to our temptation each time. To be healed, we must trust in God's mercy but also have a brother who reaches out a hand to lift us up. Faith is necessary, but we must act on that faith. We must take the hand of a brother, and we must rise even when crippled by sin to receive healing.

Will you reach out for help?
John 5:1-9, Luke 8:47-48, Luke 11:8-10, Matthew 7:8

MARCH 31

Text: *Numbers 21:2: If you will deliver these people into our hands, we will totally destroy their cities.*

God did, and they did. God's word shows me the commitment I must make in my own life. "These people" in this verse represent, to me, the enemy. Sin is the enemy of my soul and is the enemy of God. I cannot win the battle with the sin in my life, but God certainly can. It is my responsibility, though, to deliver the sin to God in the same way that it was the responsibility of the people in this verse to deliver their enemy to God. And so, Lord, I say that if you will deliver me from the sin, I will totally destroy its "cities," the places in my life where the sin dwells. God commands nothing less and expects nothing less. Other times in the history of God's people, He shows anger when the enemy is not totally destroyed. Unless sin in my life is completely destroyed, it will grow strong again and devastate me. I must be accountable to God to totally destroy the sin, for if I do not, the consequence will be that the sin will return even stronger, and the battle will continue.

Will you destroy the sin in your life?
1 John 3:9, Romans 6:12-14, Romans 13:13-14, Isaiah 55:7

APRIL

APRIL 1

Text: *2 Chronicles 12:8: They will, however, become subject to him, so that they may learn the difference between serving me and serving the kings of other lands.*

Rehaboam had led God's people into sin, rebellion, and the worship of other gods. The Lord sent a mighty army to destroy them, to take their lives, and to devastate their nation. But God's people repented and God relented. There was, however, a lesson they had to learn. The power that they had exercised was taken from them by the enemy. Their treasure was stolen, and they were no longer a free people but rather served a foreign nation. These were the consequences of their disobedience, even after they repented of their sin and were forgiven. I have repented of my sins, and I have been forgiven, but the consequences of my sins have been allowed to remain, and I must deal with them because I am accountable for my own actions. Just as God's people had a lesson to learn, so have I. Teach me Lord, but watch over me with your grace and mercy.

> *What are the consequences of your sin?*
> *Galatians 6:7-8, Proverbs 5:22, Isaiah 59:2, 2 Peter 2:4-9*

APRIL 2

Text: *2 Chronicles 24:17: But after the death of Jehoida the officials of Judah came and paid homage to the king and he listened to them.*

Jehoida brought the counsel of God to the king of Judah for all the years that he lived. And during all those years the king led wisely and well. When Jehoida died, the rulers and officials of Judah were ready for a little relaxing of the rules--a little fun in their lives. They remembered the "good old days," and how it used to be when they lived in sin. The problem was that they remembered only the sin and not the consequences. The king had never experienced the sin, for he had been only seven years old when he took the throne, and Jehoida had come along side of him, and so he listened to the rulers and officials of Judah. I have lived in freedom from my sin, and I must not return to the "good old days." Lord, help me not to remember my sin, but never let me forget the consequences.

Do you change the rules?
Psalm 119-133-134, John 14:23-24, Proverbs 10:17, 1 Peter 1:14-16

APRIL 3

Text: *Nehemiah 10:29: …and are taking on themselves a curse and an oath to walk in God's law… (NASB)*

God's people were serious about their obligation to be obedient. They not only took an oath to follow the law, they took upon themselves a curse if they were to turn away from the law. I'm not sure if I have the courage to do that, as I am so aware of my weakness. But I know, Lord, that I don't have to call a curse upon myself. You do not require it and, in fact, it is not necessary. If I fail to walk with you, if I fall away, I will lose fellowship with you and that is the greatest curse of all. I don't want to obey you because of fear of a curse. I want to obey you because you are my Father and I love you. A curse won't keep me accountable. Your love will.

Why do you obey?
Psalm 28:1, James 1:25, 1 John 2:16-17, Exodus 19:5

APRIL 4

Text: *Habakkuk 3:18: …Yet I will rejoice in the Lord, I will be joyful in God my savior.*

I t was a time in which God was about to visit judgment on an unfaithful nation and a rebellious people. Habakkuk, a prophet, knew full well what was to befall his people, and he prays for mercy in the midst of judgment. But he goes on to say that he will "accept" whatever God does, and he doesn't try to talk God out of it. He does not pray that his nation would be able to hide from or shirk God's justice, or that it would pass them by or even that his own family would be spared. He commits to rejoice in the Lord no matter what happens. Lord, in the consequences of my sin let me rejoice in you, in your salvation, and in your saving grace that has brought about my deliverance.

Will you rejoice in adversity?

Philippians 4:4-7. 1 Peter 4:12-14, Acts 16:22-25, Romans 5:3-5

APRIL 5

Text: *Zechariah 7:13: "When I called, they did not listen; so when they called, I would not listen," says the Lord almighty.*

G od's children cry out for deliverance, but their cries fall upon the ears of God who will not hear them. God is not a God who exists to serve his people; but rather, God's people have been created to serve their God. The people had become selfish, concerned only about their own needs. When God called to his people, to bring them back into obedience and a right relationship to Him, they listened not. And so, they suffered the consequences of their disobedience. Should they have expected God to listen to their pleas? Should I? I am no different from the people of Zechariah's time, but God does have mercy, and opens His ear to me when I truly repent.

Will God listen to your prayer?

Malachi 2:2, Proverbs 16:20, Psalm 116:1, 1 Peter 3:12

APRIL 6

Text: *Psalm 7:16: His mischief will return upon his own head, and his violence will descend upon his own pate.*

What we sow, so shall we reap. It is not God punishing us for our sin, but rather a universal law. It is a fundamental rule by which everything in the universe is governed. It works in nature. If you throw a ball into the air, the consequence will be that the ball will return to Earth. If you plant a seed in the ground, a plant grows. If you eat too much, you will gain weight. When there are bad consequences, we don't want to be responsible--but we are. When the ball breaks a window on its way back to Earth, or the seed produces a weed, or we become obese, it is our nature to look around for someone else to blame. But facts are facts, and consequences inevitably follow our actions. Why then are we surprised that when we sin our lives fall apart? Why do we blame God for the results of our own actions? God created us not to sin but to honor Him. If we do not use what is given us according to the maker's instructions, why are we surprised when it doesn't work well?

> *Do you accept the consequences of your sin?*
> *Galatians 6:7, Proverbs 6:27-28, Ezekiel 18:20, Romans 14:12*

APRIL 7

Text: *John 8:51: I tell you the truth, if anyone keeps my word he will never see death. "*

My salvation is God's gift to me; my obedience is my gift to him. It must be a gift that I give of my own free will. If I were not to give this gift of obedience to God, he would not exclude me from salvation, but I would surely exclude myself from everlasting life as surely as if I had refused his gift of salvation. If I choose to live a life of disobedience, my actions show that I have indeed refused his gift of salvation, for the gift is not just a reservation in heaven, but a living gift that I am to walk in, in this life. My gift to God, therefore, is nothing more than accepting the gift that He has given to me and living obediently in His gift.

Are you obedient?

John 14:15, Romans 2:5-8, 1 John 2:15-17, Luke 6:46

APRIL 8

Text: *Ecclesiastes 12:13: …fear God and keep his commandments, for this is the whole duty of man.*

My duty is twofold. First, it is to fear God, to revere Him, to stand in awe of who He is, to understand that He is God and I am only a man that He created. Second, I must obey. God's word does not tell me that I am to obey because I fear God. The word says that I am first to fear Him, then to obey his commandments. It is only when I know who God is, and who I am, that I see the reason for obedience. I must love first, that I may obey. I must obey in love and awe and respect--in holy fear.

Do you fear God?
Proverbs 8:13, Psalm 103:10-12, 1 Peter 1:17, 1 John 4:18

APRIL 9

Text: *Deuteronomy 4:1: And now, O Israel, listen to the statutes and judgments which I am teaching you to perform, in order that you may live and go in and take possession of the land the God of your fathers is giving to you.*

Moses speaks God's word to his people as they are about to enter the promised land at the end of their forty-year trek through the desert. God's word is very clear. It is just as clear for me today. God shows me in

His word, and words, the laws that I am to keep. He shows me that I am not to turn back to the old gods, and that they were not really gods at all. He shows me that if I choose to turn back, I will lose the life He has given to me and I will be driven out of the land, chosen by God, in which I am to live. I have a choice. I can return to the gods of the flesh if I wish but, if I do, I will surely lose the one true God in my life, and I will lose the inheritance He has chosen for me and for the generations to come. I must be obedient, with God's help, to His law.

What have you got to lose?

Luke 9:23-25, 1 Corinthians 3:12-15, Philippians 3:7-8, Ephesians 4:22-24

APRIL 10

Text: *Judges 10:16: Then they got rid of the foreign gods among them.*

It was a time when God's people turned from God to foreign gods, and He lifted His hand of protection from His people. The people repented of their sin, saying to God that they knew they had sinned; and yet, still God left them to the gods to which they had turned. God's heart was not softened toward them until they did something about their sin, until they rid themselves of the sin in their lives. Only then did His mighty hand of protection return to His people. We, God's people today, do the same thing. We know we are caught in sin and we truly repent. We lament over what we do and seek God's blessing and His touch, but we do not destroy the idols in our lives. Lord, your hand will not rest upon us, upon me, until we destroy the idols. We must get rid of the foreign gods among us.

Do your idols separate you from God?

Ezekiel 14:6-8, Exodus 20:2-3, Isaiah 59:2, Acts 3:19

APRIL 11

Text: *2 Samuel 8:14: The Lord gave David victory wherever he went.*

D avid decided where he would go, against whom he would war and what he would do. God gave him victory in all his decisions. But not long before these successes, David had been chased by his enemies and made no decisions for a significant period of his life, except where to hide. But here he is, no longer just fighting for his survival, but making decisions from strength. God allowed him to go through the times of being oppressed before he entered the times of victory. It was in the oppression that David learned to trust God, to listen to Him and to obey. Now, having learned the lesson, he is blessed by God. Lord, let it even be so with me, that I may learn to listen and obey, and you will give me victory.

> *Are you learning?*
> *2 Timothy 3:16-17, Hebrews 5:13-14, Ephesians 4:12-15, James 1:2-4*

APRIL 12

Text: *1 Chronicles 22:13: Then you shall prosper, if you are careful to observe the statutes and the ordinances which the Lord commanded Moses concerning Israel.*

G od gave the commands through Moses. God's people thought they were laws that they had to follow to prove their obedience. The disobedient deliberately flouted the laws. Those who wanted to appear to be obedient found loopholes in the laws, or broke the laws in the secret places of their hearts. We are no better; I am no better. But God's word says that the law is in place, so that if we follow it we will prosper. I must understand, Lord; we must understand, and be obedient in the secret places of our hearts.

> *Do you hide lawlessness?*

Matthew 15:19-20, Isaiah 29:15, John 3:20, Psalm 90:8

APRIL 13

Text: *2 Chronicles 25:2: He did what was right in the eyes of the Lord, but not whole-heartedly.*

Amaziah's problem was that he knew what he should do. He was obedient--up to a point. But his heart wasn't really in it. He was obedient because he knew he should be, but the rebellion within him coveted disobedience. It would have been better if he had not known right from wrong, because he could certainly have done "wrong" wholeheartedly. When the Lord blessed him with victory, he brought other gods to worship because that is what half-hearted obedience does. Lord, help me to do what is right with all my might, all my soul, and all my mind. Don't let me be half-hearted.

Is your heart right with God?
Mark 12:30, Psalm 119:10-11, Jeremiah 23:13, Matthew 22:37

APRIL 14

Text: *Ezekiel 33:12: The righteousness of the righteous man will not save him when he disobeys, and the wickedness of the wicked man will not cause him to fall when he turns from it.*

The Lord does not delight in punishment, nor does he hold offense in the face of repentance. But God must be obeyed. Past sin will not keep me from God today if I renounce my sin and turn to Him, and all the times that I have walked with Him will not bridge the chasm created by my sin today. It is obedience, today, in this moment, that God desires. Even today,

I must choose the path that I will tread. I will walk toward God or away from God. The choice is mine.

Who do you choose today?
Deuteronomy 30:19, Romans 8:13, Matthew 6:24, Joshua 24:15

APRIL 15

Text: *Luke 5:11: So they pulled their boats up on shore, left everything, and followed him.*

Peter and his partners were not having a good day. They had fished all night and caught nothing, and here comes Jesus to their bit of beach. Peter probably had been looking forward to a nap. But Jesus' words drew him, and Jesus even asked to use his boat as a speaker's platform. So, when Jesus told him to fish again, he was skeptical. He was skeptical but obedient. So, he fished and hit the mother lode, more fish than he would have caught in a week or even in a month. His business got the boost it needed. He was on his way to success. But then, Jesus called him, and he left his catch on the beach, all the delights of the world, to be obedient to Jesus and to follow Him. Me too, Lord.

What keeps you from following Jesus?
Hebrews 12:1, 1 John 2:15-17, Luke 12:34, Mark 10:29-30

APRIL 16

Text: *Hebrews 1:9: You have loved righteousness and hated wickedness.*

God does love righteousness and He does hate wickedness. This, alone, should be enough to compel me to avoid sin and to make sure that all my actions are righteous. But simply doing the things that God wants me to do and avoiding sin, because it is His will, is not enough. God has commanded that I learn to be like Him, and I must learn to be like Him not only in my actions but also in my heart. If my actions are righteous, and my wickedness is put aside, and yet in my heart I discard righteousness and love sin, then I have failed God. Lord, make me like you: change my heart.

Do you love righteousness?

Psalm 34:15, Matthew 5:6, Proverbs 21:21, Isaiah 48:18

APRIL 17

Text: *Galatians 3:21: For if a law had been given that could impart life, then righteousness would certainly have come by the law.*

The law tells us how to act. It tells us what we must do and what we must not. It is the framework of our behavior. But it does not touch the heart, and sooner or later the heart will dictate my behavior. I can obey the law to the letter and yet hold rebellion in my heart and, when that happens, I will bend the law to my heart's desire or eventually abandon the law altogether. My heart, then, is healed by the Holy Spirit and by Jesus' death on the cross that I might, and must, obey the law out of reverence for God and His precious gift to me. I can no longer obey the law out of obligation and fear, but rather I must obey out of the desire of my heart to be righteous.

Is your obedience from your heart?

Psalm 119:24, John 14:15, 2 John 1:6, 1 John 5:3-4

APRIL 18

Text: *Psalm 1:2: But his delight is in the law of the Lord, and in his law he meditates day and night.*

Sometimes, Lord, I follow your law reluctantly. I obey because I must, not because I want to. Sometimes I stand obedient to your law, but I look out at the lawlessness and wickedness, and the temptations draw my heart and my desire to evil. Sometimes I have fallen and, when I fall, it is then that I realize that I am away from you, and I desire to come to you and be in communion with you again, because when I am with you, I am truly delighted. And so, I return in repentance and forgiveness, and I again think about your law and how good it is to be safe in you. Lord, to really follow your will, to think about you as I go through my day, to discover you in the little occurrences and in the people I see, this is my delight. When I do this, when I truly follow you, Lord, I know that you delight in me.

> *What will bring you delight?*
> *1 Corinthians 13:6-7, Proverbs 11:20, Psalm 119:35, Psalm 37:3-4*

APRIL 19

Text: *Psalm 119:9: How can a young man keep his way pure? By living according to your word.*

In order to keep my way pure, I must begin in purity. I cannot keep my way pure when I reside in a state of impurity. I must, therefore, confess and repent at the beginning and receive the cleansing of the Holy Spirit. Once this is accomplished, I must live according to God's word. I must hide it within my mind and heart so that it is present all day long. It is not enough to know the word. It is not enough to understand it. I must guard my life from doing all those things that are not in accord with the word. I must, each day, abide in God's word, his precepts, and his laws. The word must be my residence. It cannot be, nor was it ever intended to be, a post office box.

Does God's word abide in you?
John 15:4-5, Matthew 4:4, 1 John 2:5-6, John 15:9-11

APRIL 20

Text: *Luke 6:46: Why do you call me Lord, Lord, and do not do what I say?*

If I acknowledge that there is one God, and I understand that my Lord has set down rules, not to deprive me, but so that my life might be blessed and so I might be a blessing to others, why, then, do I do those things that God has told me I must not do? It is a spirit of lawlessness and rebellion. I am once again a child, even though I am now old, who desires to assert my independence from my parents on whom I depended. I desire to do things my way, to indulge the temptations of the flesh because I can, because my mind and my spirit have told me that even if I disobey I "surely will not die." If I continue to sin, I must not call my heavenly Father "Lord" but, rather, I will have to call the sin and rebellion "lord."

Who do you call Lord?
Matthew 7:21-23, Judges 2:12-13, Acts 7:39-40, Psalm 40:4

APRIL 21

Text: *Jeremiah 16:19: O Lord, my strength and my fortress, my refuge in time of distress...*

Only in the Lord is my strength. During this time of recovery, He has told me and He has shown me that He did not make me physically powerful. Had He done so, I would be more tempted to take credit for the healing that God has accomplished in my life, and I would, I'm sure, boast in my own strength. But now I know that I need no strength but His, for God will keep me and will keep my family from harm with His great and mighty arm. I thank God for my weakness, and for His strength.

Are you weak enough?

1 Corinthians 1:27, 2 Corinthians 12:9-10, Romans 8:26, Isaiah 40:29-31

APRIL 22

Text: *Deuteronomy 9:4: After the Lord your God has driven them out before you, do not say to yourself "the Lord has brought me here to take possession of this land because of my righteousness."*

Just as with the tribes, God has brought me out of the desert of my addiction and given me possession of the land where I may dwell in peace. I know there is still a lot of desert in me, but I am now finally living where God intended me to dwell. I confess that I am tempted, on occasion, to say, "Look what I have done," when I have done nothing at all. God has done it in me. I tried for half a century to do it myself and failed every time I tried. When I finally cried out to God and surrendered it to Him and truly desired to leave the desert, God rescued me. It is nothing that I have done. It is all about God's grace and His blessing upon me. May I never forget that! May I never think or believe that I did this by myself. Thank you, Lord, for the greener pastures.

Are you trying to heal yourself?

Romans 5:6, 1 Peter 2:24, 1 Corinthians 10:13, Psalm 30:2

APRIL 23

Text: *2 Chronicles 32:26: Then Hezekiah repented of the pride of his heart, as did the people of Jerusalem, therefore the Lord's wrath did not come upon them during the days of Hezekiah.*

After all that God had done for him, Hezekiah became proud. God had saved him from the powerfully evil Sennacherab by a miracle. God brought Hezekiah and the people into obedience and faithfulness as they destroyed the false gods in their land. God revealed to them that He was, in fact, the only true God. Much had been accomplished, and as Hezekiah became proud of what had been done so did his people, so that his pride and the pride of the people threatened all that had been accomplished in the nation. After all that God has done in my life, I cannot allow pride to jeopardize His work, His cleansing, His restoration. If there be any pride in me, I confess that now, and I repent.

In what do you take pride?
1 Timothy 6:17, James 1:9-11, Proverb 11:2, Psalm 10:4

APRIL 24

Text: *Ezra 8:22: The gracious hand of our God is on everyone who looks to him, but his great anger is against all who forsake him.*

This was the boast made by Ezra before King Atarxerxes. Now, Ezra faced a real challenge. He was about to set out on a journey with only a small band of men for protection. They were heavily laden with tons of silver and gold. Their treasure would be obvious to anyone who chose to watch them. They would not be able to travel quickly or to outrun or outfight thieves hungry for plunder or enemy nations through which they were to pass. But the boast of the Lord had been made, and now Ezra could not ask for protection from Atarxerxes. And so, Ezra prayed. In the journey that I have undertaken, let me boast of the Lord, so that I cannot rely on the strength of my right arm or the people of the world to protect me, but rather that I will pray and lean upon God alone.

Who protects you?

Jeremiah 17:5, Proverbs 3:5-6, Psalm 20:7, Philippians 4:19

APRIL 25

Text: *Proverbs 29:23: A man's pride will bring him low. But a humble spirit will obtain honor.*

Pride, basically, is me presenting myself to the world as something better than I really am. Humility is presenting myself to the world as who I really am. As I continue my walk in my recovery, there will be moments of failure. There will be slips, issues, and problems. If I am prideful, I will deny any problems and, when asked how I am doing, I will deny that there are still temptations or problems. If I am humble, I will admit the temptations and slips in my life and allow my brothers to strengthen me in the battle. My pride will make me afraid of what my brothers will say, and it will surely set me up for a fall. If I am humble, I will be treated with kindness by my brothers and will be raised up and exalted by God and man.

Do you hide your sin from your brothers?

Isaiah 29:15, John 3:20-21, James 5:16, Galatians 6:2

APRIL 26

Text: *Psalm 21:13: Be exalted, O Lord, in your strength; we will sing and praise your might.*

It is God's strength that protects and blesses me and overcomes the temptations of the flesh and all of the enticements that the enemy holds out to me. I have tried to overcome the world in my own strength. God has blessed me with a strong right arm, yet I am weak compared to the armies of the enemy. He has blessed me with a fine mind, yet I am outmaneuvered and tricked almost daily by the world and the enemy. I have been blessed with a powerful will, and yet my attempts to white knuckle the times of temptation and to "just say no" have been abject failures. It is only in the strength of God, and not in any of my strength, that I am safe. And so, I rejoice in the strength of God, and I will sing and praise His might.

> *Do you think you are stronger than God?*
> *Psalm 28:7-8, 2 Corinthians 12:9-10, 1 Corinthians 1:27, Genesis 1:1*

APRIL 27

Text: *Psalm 70:5: Yet I am poor and needy; come quickly to me, O God. You are my help and my deliverer; O Lord, do not delay.*

Lord, I confess to you that I am poor and needy. Sometimes, Lord, in this struggle that I go through, as I battle the flesh, I come to a place of protection where I am doing well. I know, Lord, that it is your mighty hand that allows me to be protected. But Lord, I must catch myself in those times because my pride rises up and says, "See how well I am doing!" and I am tempted to credit my own strength. Lord, even then, especially then, I am poor and needy. I implore you, Lord, come quickly in those times. Surround me, that I might not fall. It is in the good times that I must be reminded of my total dependence on you. You and only you can keep me in your will, walking obediently.

Do you take God's grace for granted?

Ephesians 2:4, James 4:6, 1 John 1:8-10, Romans 6:1-2

APRIL 28

Text: *Acts 9:34: …Jesus Christ heals you…*

Lord, as of this moment, I get it. I will stop trying to heal myself. I will stop trying not to sin. At least I will stop trying to heal myself in my own strength. I cannot heal myself. I cannot abstain from sin. I know because I have tried and failed and temptation keeps threatening to overwhelm me. But, Lord, YOU can heal me. YOU can strengthen me to stand against the enemy when I am tempted. I can't do it, Lord. Only YOU can do it for me. Thank you, Lord.

Who keeps you from sin?

1 Corinthians 10:13, Romans 13:14, Galatians 5:16, 1 John 1:9

APRIL 29

Text: *Numbers 15: 39: …and so you will remember all the commands of the Lord, that you may obey them and not prostitute yourselves by going after the lusts of your own hearts and eyes.*

When I disobey the Lord, I make of myself a prostitute. A prostitute is a person who sells their body and their soul for a few dollars, the symbol of a world of greed. Earlier in this same chapter God tells us that all people are held to the same standard--God's people and the "aliens" among us. Whenever we are disobedient to God's law, we become prostitutes selling our souls and our relationship to the world for a moment of pleasure, for a modicum of control, for a flattering glance. We sell our eternal relationship to God, piece by piece, sin by sin, for moments of gratification in our brief lives here on Earth. Help me, Lord, not to be a prostitute before you but rather to be your bride, pure and spotless on the day that you call me to you for the last time.

Who owns you?
Romans 12:1, Matthew 6:24, Romans 6:17, Joshua 24:15

April 30

Text: *Joshua 6:18: But as for you, only keep yourselves from the things under the ban, lest you covet them…*

God's command was that when He gave His people victory over the enemy, they were to destroy everything that they found in the enemy camp. I don't think that the possessions of the enemy were necessarily evil, but God knew that His people would "covet" the plunder. God also knew that the covetousness would become a habit, and that His people would begin waging war on their own to get "stuff" instead of waging war to get the land that He had promised them. The people would be drawn away from worshipping Him, to worshiping Earthly treasure. I am engaged in a spiritual war, and I must not covet the "stuff" of the enemy, the power of the enemy, the advantages that the world offers here on Earth, or the ease of the enemy's life in this world. Lord, let me destroy all that is of the enemy.

What in the world do you want?
1 John 2:15-16, Galatians 5:16-17, Matthew 4:4, Matthew 16:26

MAY

MAY 1

Text: *2 Samuel 11:1: But David remained in Jerusalem.*

The kings went out to war, but David stayed home. David had too much time on his hands. He was bored. He was in a place that God did not intend for him to be. Because he was not busy, because he was bored, because he was not doing what God intended him to do, he fell into serious sin. The enemy always seems to provide opportunity for my flesh during the times that I am lazy and bored. My mind, not concentrated on what I should be thinking of, defaults to thinking of the flesh, and the enemy creates a myriad of ways for me to fall into sin. The Sin always starts first in my mind. I have fallen before because of the boredom, because I was not where God wanted me to be, and not doing what God had for me to do. Help me, Lord, to stay focused on you and your plans for me, and to fight against the laziness and boredom.

> *Do you provide opportunity for sin?*
> *Ephesians 5:15-20, 1 Thessalonians 5:14, Proverbs 15:19, Proverbs 13:4*

MAY 2

Text: *John 3:20: Everyone who does evil hates the light, and will not come into the light for fear that his deeds will be exposed.*

I am a liar when I am tempted, and I allow fleshly temptations to enter my life, and yet proclaim God as my king. I am a hypocrite when I say that I love God but hide the darkness in my life from God's light, protecting the dark corners of my soul from truth. But God knows and loves me in spite of my hypocrisy. He is leading me out of the darkness and into the light. He leads me away from the lure of the flesh and the temptations that I hide. One by one, moment by moment, day by day, I walk more and more in His light. I will never be totally free of temptation unless God chooses to make me completely free. But I will look to the light as God frees me, one temptation at a time.

Are you sheltering temptation?

Romans 13:14, 1 Peter 5:8-9, Psalm 119:11, James 1:13-15

MAY 3

Text: *John 19:10: "Do you refuse to speak to me?" Pilate said. "Don't you realize I have power either to free you or to crucify you?"*

So, there He was, my Lord, Jesus. He had been tortured all night, mocked, and ridiculed, torn down, physically, mentally, and emotionally. He knew what lay ahead, and his body was screaming at him to stop the torture. Now was the time that Satan looked and saw what was happening to Jesus, and he was certain that this was the time to hit him with temptation again. And so, he offered Jesus a way out. What Satan could not know was that although Jesus' body was broken, His spirit, the very spirit of God, remained intact. Jesus would not be tempted. The same spirit lives in me and gives me the strength to withstand whatever temptation the enemy brings. Jesus died that I might have the power to withstand the temptation of the enemy. I must resolve that I will resist temptation in the power of God's spirit.

Will you resist temptation?

Matthew 26:41, 1 Corinthians 10:13, James 4:7, Galatians 5:16-17

MAY 4

Text: *Romans 1:28: Furthermore, since they did not think it worthwhile to retain the knowledge of God, he gave them over to a depraved mind, to do what ought not to be done.*

Here I am, a Christian, a disciple of Jesus. I have learned of my Lord, I know Jesus; I have studied God's word. Yet, the world offers perversity, and calls me to look upon evil. It sends temptations and sorrows to occupy my mind. I dwell not upon, nor in, Jesus and His Holy Word, but in the things of the world. God tells me that if my mind is consumed with fleshly comforts and worldly temptations, He will let me have what I desire, and I will be lost in the maelstrom of worldly thoughts and desires. Lord, if I am to be free of my sin, I must dwell in and upon you.

> *Where do your thoughts dwell?*
> *Philippians 4:8, 2 Corinthians 10:5, Colossians 3:2-3, Isaiah 26:3*

MAY 5

Text: *Colossians 1:11: …strengthened with all power, according to his glorious might, for the attaining of all steadfastness and patience…*

Like all of us, I sometimes feel the pull of the world's temptation so strongly that I literally believe I cannot hold out against it. I am not alone in this, of course. I believe that no matter what the temptation is, we all feel that same draw. And we are right; we cannot resist. We have not the power. Our God, however, expects us to mature in holiness. He expects us to be steadfast in our battle against our addictions and patient in purity as we conform our lives to His. Is it unfair of God to expect this, since we cannot resist? It would be unfair if not for Christ's death and resurrection, which gives us His power to resist. His power and glorious might are more than enough to enable us to resist, if we choose to allow His power to work in us. God wins, if we let Him.

Can you resist temptation?

2 Corinthians 10:3-5, Galatians 5:16-17, Psalm 119:9-10, Romans 6:14

MAY 6

Text: *1 Thessalonians 4:7: For God did not call us to be impure, but to live a holy life.*

We have all been called by God. Some answer; some do not. But for those of us who answer, what is the call? Is it not to live a holy life? My body wars against the call. Impurity and the attraction of lust tempt me to turn a deaf ear to the call that I have heard and answered, and instead to satisfy the yearning of the flesh that somehow never seems to disappear. Sometimes it seems that the urges are so strong that I must allow my desire to prevail. But God will not, and does not, call us to the impossible. If God has called me to a holy life, He can, and will, and does give me the power to live that life. I must trust Him and allow Him to lead me to the life that He promises.

To what has God called you?

1 Peter 5:10, 1 Timothy 6:12, 1 Peter 1:14-16, Ephesians 4:1

MAY 7

Text: *Hebrews 2:18: Because he himself suffered when he was tempted, he is able to help those who are being tempted.*

Jesus was not the sheltered, pampered child, protected from the world, knowing no temptation. Jesus knew and suffered every temptation that I suffer; only I'm quite sure that Satan preyed upon Jesus much more diligently than he seeks after me. Jesus never fell; Jesus never gave in to temptation; Jesus never sinned. When I am tempted, when I stand stripped of my good intentions and firm resolutions, teetering on the brink of disobedience, Jesus promises to come and guide me to safety if I will turn to Him and ask for help. Jesus will not dwell with me when I choose to live in sin, but He will never fail to come for me no matter where I am if I reach out for Him.

Do you ask for help when tempted?

1 John 5:14-15, Psalm 120:1, Romans 6:13, Psalm 34:17

MAY 8

Text: *Proverbs 1:10: My son, if sinners entice you do not give in to them.*

I am enticed by sin and by sinners. Enticement is the lure of the unknown, the temptation of the forbidden. It is an attraction to my eye and a draw upon my mind. When someone tells me "no," that I may not do something, then my rebellious self raises up and says, "I can if I want." My mind questions why I am not allowed to do that which I wish to do. Those who are already involved in the sin are those I usually find to be attractive. They are often charming, they are "cool," and they not only promise pleasure but fellowship as well. And I, like a little bird, eye the seed in the fowler's trap with curiosity and jealousy and fleshly hunger. I inch ever closer to the snare, by which I will come to the most miserable of all states in my life. I may eat the seed, but at what cost? Strengthen me, Lord.

Do you rebel against God's word?

Luke 6:46, James 1:22, Psalm 107:10-11, Proverbs 28:9

MAY 9

Text: *Proverbs 9:17-18: Stolen water is sweet; food eaten in secret is delicious! But little do they know that the dead are there, that her guests are in the depths of the grave.*

It all looks so good from the outside as I do a "drive by" looking at sin. There's the enemy, sitting in front of a palatial mansion, offering illicit temptations. Stolen fruit, promising a taste of what belongs to someone else, tells me that because it is not mine it is ever so much sweeter, so much better. Stolen water will surely slake my thirst that the enemy brought upon me in the first place. But the water turns to brine. It is like driving by a wealthy and beautiful funeral home, not knowing what it is, and thinking that it would be a wonderful place to live, never realizing that it is not a place for the living but a beautiful edifice for the dead. It is a façade. It looks good only from the outside. Wisdom warns me of the death that awaits.

> *Are you attracted to sin?*
> *Proverbs 7:21-22, Genesis 3:6, 1 John 2:15-17, James 1:13-15*

MAY 10

Text: *Proverbs 29:6: An evil man is snared by his own sin, but a righteous one can sing and be glad.*

See the bird as it walks willingly into the snare of the fowler. It is wary, nervous, knowing that the treat placed on the ground in the midst of the trap is not in the right order of things and should not be there. But it is so tempting, and even knowing that it is not right, the bird goes ahead and the trap is sprung and the bird is taken captive to be sold and to live the rest of its life in a cage, or perhaps eaten or destroyed. See the bird that resists the trap perched on a limb, flitting from branch to branch, singing its tune and ruffling its feathers, happy and secure that all is right in its world. I can be whichever bird I choose to be. Sin is the bait that Satan uses in his snare, and I know that it is not in the right order of things. Let me sing and be glad.

Do you choose freedom?

Galatians 5:1, Psalm 119:45, Luke 4:18-19, Romans 6:22-23

MAY 11

Text: *Psalm 121:7: The Lord will protect you from all evil; he will keep your soul. (NASB)*

My Lord will protect me from the addiction that I face. He will keep me from it and keep my soul pure and clean. He will guard my eyes and my mind. But God will only protect me if I let Him. He has given me free choice. When times of temptation come, and they will come, I must choose to stay in God's protective hand or jump into the fiery hands of the enemy. God says that He will protect me. He does not say that He will remove all temptation. If He was to do so, He would have to remove free choice, and I would then be a robot living in a world of automatons. No! Satan has been given the power to tempt me but not the power to win. I have been given the power to win if I choose to turn to God's power and protection.

Will you choose temptation?

1 Corinthians 10:13, Proverbs 7:25-26, James 1:12, Hebrews 11:24-25

MAY 12

Text: *Psalm 124:7: We have escaped like a bird out of the fowler's snare; the snare has been broken and we have escaped.*

L ord, I was in the fowler's snare, and I stepped into it willingly, eagerly, for the few morsels that had been laid there as bait. It was so attractive to the eye, and I was so concerned about my own wants and desires that I took a step toward the tempting bait. Then I took another step, and another, and before long I was racing into the snare that I might satisfy my greed and hunger with the promises of the enemy. But you intervened, Lord. Even as I stood in the trap, even as I was in the midst of my feeding frenzy, you led me out of the trap and then you broke the trap. The snare is gone. Thank you, Lord, for your goodness to me.

> *What snare is before you?*
> *Psalm 141:9-10, 1 Peter 5:8, 2 Timothy 2:25-26, Psalm 31:4-5*

MAY 13

Text: *Proverbs 11:22: As a ring of gold in a swine's snout, so is a beautiful woman who lacks discretion.*

I look at her and admire her beautiful form, her very body, and she thinks nothing of revealing much of her body to anyone who happens to pass by. Perhaps she is the woman I stare at in the magazine I should never have opened, or the woman who shamelessly enters into a sexual performance on the internet or on a DVD. Perhaps she is the prostitute, or the strip club dancer and, yes, her body is beautiful and seductive, and I think to myself how sexy she is. What I am really thinking is what it would be like to have sexual relations with her. She has allowed me to see her and to be drawn in.

Her beauty is the gold ring, but the temptation and the contemplation of what could happen is ugly. I become a pig in a mud bath, eating garbage. I must instead seek after real gold-- my relationship to God.

What are you looking at?

Matthew 6:22-23, Psalm 101:3, Matthew 5:28, 2 Peter 2:14

MAY 14

Text: *Luke 22:40: Pray that you will not fall into temptation.*

Jesus is about to die. Why does He choose this moment to tell his followers to pray that they may not fall? First, I believe, because He knew that they would soon be without His physical presence. Second, He knew that Satan would really go after them to keep them from going on with the Lord, as Satan thought he had been successful in ridding the world of Jesus. This was to be Satan's time, or so Satan thought. What did Jesus pray? He did not pray that there would be no temptation: He knew there would be. He did not pray that the temptation would be taken away or that His followers would not have to struggle with it. Jesus prayed that they would not fall. And so, I pray, knowing I will face temptations each day, and that they will not go away. I pray that I will not fall.

Will you fall?

Psalm 37:23-24, Isaiah 41:13, Proverbs 4:11-12, 1 Corinthians 10:13

MAY 15

Text: *Isaiah 24:21: In that day the Lord will punish the powers in the heavens above and the kings on the earth below.*

Lord, your promise is too much for me. It unravels me. You, oh Lord, will mete out justice, not only to the rulers of this world but also to powers and principalities that oppose you. And here am I, a pathetic, small voice that says, "I love you," even though I often do not act as if I care about you at all. In that day, the Day of Judgment, Lord, please remember my voice and forget my sin, that you would not be required in your perfect justice to come against me with your might. I do truly repent and run to the sheltering blood of the lamb.

> *Do your actions show that you love God?*
> *1 John 3:18, Titus 1:16, Matthew 7:21, James 1:22*

MAY 16

Text: *Psalm 128:1: Blessed are all who fear the Lord, who walk in his ways.*

I fear you, Lord. I do not fear what your wrath will do to me because I know your kindness, and I have accepted what Jesus did on the cross that my sin might be forgiven. I know that you love me and that you will always be my Father. What I fear, Lord, is what my sin will do when it drives me away from your holiness. I fear walking through this world alone, without you by my side. Bless me Father by making me afraid of losing your presence in my life. Bless me by making me afraid of walking away from you.

> *Do you fear separation from God?*
> *Isaiah 59:2, Hebrews 3:12-13, Acts 3:19, Romans 11:22*

MAY 17

Text: *Numbers 14:11: How long will these people treat me with contempt?*

The Lord spoke clearly to His people. He told them that He was giving them the Promised Land. He let them see the abundance of the land that He had set aside for them, but they would not claim God's gift to them because of their fear of the world. In essence they were saying that the enemy was stronger than God. In fact, they did treat God with contempt. They were given a choice of facing their enemies in the world, with God by their side, or facing the wrath of the enemy alone. Clearly, the world would not become their friend. I face the same choice. Oftentimes, I know God's command, but I am afraid of the enemy in the world. I choose to flee from what God wants for me, because I think it is too hard. Is anything too hard with God on my side? Lord, let me not treat you with contempt.

> *What in the world are you afraid of?*
> *Psalm 23:4, Matthew 10:28, Psalm 118:6-7, 1 Peter 3:13-14*

MAY 18

Text: *Esther 2:7: And he was bringing up Hadassah, that is Esther, his uncle's daughter, for she had neither father nor mother.*

Lord, you are a father to the fatherless, and you choose the lost and lonely to be your very own. I had an Earthly father and mother, and they were good parents by the world's standards, and they did the best that they could. I always had enough of the worldly things as a child and discipline to keep me out of trouble. What they could not give me, because of the way in which they were raised, was the love and touch that I cried out for. They loved me and I knew, and still know, that they loved me, but they could not express it. What my father was unable to give me--his love, his touch, his heart--you have given to me, Lord. I see your love, I feel your touch, and I hear the beat of your heart. What my mother couldn't do, when she couldn't hold me, I feel in your tender touch. While my parents couldn't tell me that they loved me, I hear you saying that you love me over and over again, sometimes not only once a day but many times each day. Thank you, Lord, for bringing me up. Thank you for choosing me.

Have you felt the Father's love?
Luke 15:20, John 14:23, 1 John 3:1, Luke 3:23

MAY 19

Text: *Proverbs 1:7: The fear of the Lord is the beginning of knowledge, but fools despise wisdom and discipline.*

Am I to fear my God? The God who knows me and loves me so much that He laid down His life for me? Am I to be afraid of Him? I am to love Him and be afraid of separation from Him. I am to respect Him enough to be afraid of the consequences of not loving Him. An all-powerful God can cause great calamity in my life should He choose to do so, but He does not. Instead, He simply allows me to do that which I wish, and then He allows me to suffer the consequence of my decision. How, then, should I fear the Lord? I will fear Him through discipline and wisdom. Discipline, simply, is realizing God's will for my life on a minute-by-minute basis and then being faithful enough to obey. Wisdom is the gift of knowing what God would have me do. I will know because of His word, the voice of my conscience, and by listening to and communing with Him.

Are you afraid of God?
Psalm 33:18-19, Psalm 103-11, John 14:27, Romans 8:15-16

MAY 20

Text: *Proverbs 3:25: Do not be afraid of sudden terror, nor of trouble from the wicked when it comes... (NASB)*

But sudden terror is one of the most terrible of fears; how can I not be afraid? I must not be afraid to be afraid. Let terror come, and when it does come--when it does come to me--I will still be secure in the hand of the Lord. The wicked will surely bring trouble upon me. The verse does not say "if it comes" but rather "when it comes." One thing I can be sure of is that the wicked will bring trouble upon all that they meet, the godly and the ungodly alike. It is their perverse nature to bring trouble on others because, as they do it, this makes them feel better about their own lives. But even in this, I am secure in God's hand. After all, if I walk next to God, how can another man, also created by God, bring harm upon me?

> *Are you afraid of fear?*
> *Isaiah 35:4, Psalm 118:6, 1 Corinthians 16:13, 1 John 4:18*

MAY 21

Text: *Psalm 2:7: He said to me, "You are my son; today I have become your father."*

What was your father like? If he was human, he was imperfect, just as I was when my children lived with me. Even now I am an imperfect father. Perhaps, on balance, your father was a great father. Perhaps there is no balance, and your father was anything but a great father. Do you recall wishing that your father would change, that he would do certain things or not do certain things? Whatever he was like, do you remember trying to please him, to be the child that he would approve? There is a father who is perfect, without flaw, who will do what is best for us every time and will love us completely, no matter what we do or do not do. He is, of course, our heavenly Father--God himself. The relationship can be real, and God offers the relationship without cost. Today, he says, "You are my son…"

Are you God's child?

John 1:12-13, 2 Corinthians 6:18, Revelation 21:6-7, Galatians 4:4-7

MAY 22

Text: *Psalm 25:14: The Lord confides in those who fear him; he makes his covenant known to them.*

The Lord's word is available for all to see: it is not hidden. God does not choose that some would come to Him and some would not, but rather His word teaches that He is not willing that any perish. But God's word also says that the fear of the Lord is the beginning of wisdom. Many of us know of God's word, and some even know his word, but many have not understood his word, for they neither respect nor fear the author. Some do not keep the commands of God's words because they rely on themselves, and they rely on themselves because they do not keep his word. But to the one who fears God, and keeps his commands and relies upon the strength of God, belongs fellowship with God. He will hear God's voice as God confides in him, and he will be the child of God.

Do you heed God's word?

Hebrews 2:1, James 1:22-25, John 8:31, Matthew 4:4

MAY 23

Text: *Psalm 34:4: I sought the Lord and he answered me; he delivered me from all my fears.*

I am so fearful. I fear the enemy who preys upon my soul. I fear my flesh that cries out in the darkness to be satisfied by sin. I fear evil men who would tempt me to be part of the fellowship of sin and rebellion. I fear that my sins will be visited upon my children and grandchildren. I fear a reversal of fortune and exposure to the ridicule of those that I love. But, in the fear that comes upon me, I seek God. I do not only seek His answer to my fear. I do not only seek the protection of God's hand. I do not limit my search to God's blessing. I seek God, and He finds me and brings me deliverance from my fear. For who can be afraid in the presence of God? Then God showers me with all His other blessings. But, you, Lord, are what I seek. You are the answer.

> *Does God heal your fear?*
> *Isaiah 41:10, Psalm 94:16-19, Philippians 4:6-7, 1 Peter 5: 7*

MAY 24

Text: *Psalm 37:12&13: The wicked plot against the righteous and gnash their teeth at them, but the Lord laughs at the wicked for he knows their day is coming.*

Why am I so afraid of mankind and the evil in this world? Those who are evil seek to frighten me; they do gnash their teeth at me, and my heart trembles and my knees shake. But, why? They threaten to take my worldly goods from me—good, let them have them. My gifts come from God, not man. They threaten to harm me and to harm my family. The greatest evil they can think of would be to take my life and, if they do, I will be in paradise with my Lord for eternity. They threaten to hold me up to the scorn and ridicule of the world. Even so, I will stand proudly before my God. Very soon, both my adversary and I will stand before God. The Lord will welcome me as His brother, as His returning child, as one He loves. But my adversary, if he does not know my Lord, will experience all the emotions of fear and dismay that he has tried to bring upon me.

How can the world harm you?
2 Corinthians 12:10, Romans 8:35, Luke 23:34, Revelation 2:10

MAY 25

Text: *Psalm 56:4: In God, whose word I praise, in God I trust. I will not be afraid. What can mortal man do to me?*

The world seeks to make me afraid. They threaten me with illness, shame, poverty, and pain. They tell me that if only I will reject my God, they will make me important, wealthy and comfortable all my days. If I reject the world, the world will reject me, taking away all that the world can offer. But in you, Lord, I trust, and in your holy word. You are greater than this world. You created the world and all the people in it, and you created me. Why should I countenance the threat that your created bring against me when you love me? If you allow me life, I praise you. If I die, I praise you. What, then, can my enemy do to me?

What does the world promise to you?
1 Timothy 6:10, James 4:1-4, 1 John 2:15-17, Mark 8:36

MAY 26

Text: *Psalm 112:7: He will not fear evil tidings; his heart is steadfast, trusting in the Lord. (NASB)*

Some of us, on occasion, wake up in the morning and our first thought is, "What will God do to me today?" There are many of us who wake to addiction, in the very real fear that the enemy will be able to have his way in our lives that very day. God did not create us to live a life of fear. Surely God knows all the evils of the world that may befall us, for He has seen all things from the beginning of time and knows all things through eternity. In spite of all the danger, all the turmoil, all the temptation, God says fear not. Our hearts can be, and must be, steadfast, set, unwavering, like a rock in the middle of a storm. We must fear nothing. We must fear no one. We must know that our Lord will take care of us, no matter what.

> *Who's got your back today?*
> *Hebrews 4:16, Psalm 44:4-7, 1 John 5:14-15, Proverbs 3:5-6*

MAY 27

Text: *Job 3:25: For what I fear comes upon me, and what I dread befalls me.*

Some of us live with, or have lived with, an ever-present awareness of doom. We know that we are plagued by a sin that will kill the spirit within us and will bring us physically to ruin. We dread having to stand in God's presence and admit to the dreadful sins that we have committed. We know, no matter how deep we try to bury our sin that, as we sin, we grieve Jesus, we grieve the Spirit that God has given us, and we grieve our God. We somehow learn to live with this dread, and the belief that we will never be found worthy of salvation, because we have trampled on the gift of God. But we still fear the consequences of our sin, even though we have learned to live with it. We cannot run from it; we cannot elude it. It is a constant in our lives. The only way to overcome the fear is through earnest confession, true repentance, and walking out the freedom that only God can give to us. Then, and only then, will we experience true peace and be free of the spirit of condemnation.

Do you feel condemned?

1 John 3:19-20, Romans 8:1-4, Psalm 34:22, John 3:16-18

MAY 28

Text: *1 Chronicles 21:30: But David could not go before it to inquire of God, for he was terrified by the sword of the angel of the Lord. (NASB)*

David has sinned by taking a census. It was his pride in counting the strength of his people, even after God had told him to trust in Him and not the strength of his army. Now David admits his sin and chooses to place his punishment in the hand of God, rather than being subject to the punishment of man. God strikes the land, even though God relented when David took responsibility for his actions and the actions of his nation. God allows David to see His destroying angel and the sheer power of His punishment on David's land, and upon David and his people. The power is so great that David cannot go up to the Holy Mountain of God. David is God's friend, as we are God's friends. David loves God as we do, and God loves David even as He loves us. But David's fear is real, because God allowed David to see the power of the Lord. Lord, I need to know David's fear.

Do you fear the consequences of your sin?

Galatians 6:7-8, Matthew 7:21-23, Romans 6:23, Colossians 3:25

MAY 29

Text: *Jeremiah 31:19: After I strayed, I repented; after I came to understand, I beat my breast. I was ashamed and humiliated because I bore the disgrace of my youth.*

Just as with Ephraim, God has delivered me from the burden of shame and disgrace. He has led me out of the dark places that I cultivated in my youth and that blossomed in my later years. God has led me out of the dark places and remembers not the shadows. God remembers my face only in the light. The shame and disgrace of my youth no longer linger within me or upon me. My God has set me free from the shame, and I will walk in freedom.

> *Do you live with shame?*
> *Psalm 44:15-16, Isaiah 61:7, Psalm 31:17, Hebrews 8:12*

MAY 30

Text: *2 Peter 2:20: If they have escaped the corruption of the world by knowing our Lord and Savior, Jesus Christ, and are again entangled in it and overcome, they are worse off at the end than they were at the beginning.*

And such was I. God had provided me with a way of escape and, instead, I put on a mask of Christianity and sank ever deeper into my sin. Only this time the guilt and shame increased a hundredfold, and I was truly more miserable than I had ever been. I believed that the ever-present sin that gripped me could not be broken. I could see no avenue of escape. And then God came to me, and He delivered me, and I am free of the guilt and the sin, and the shame.

> *Can you ever be free from sin?*
> *Galatians 5:1, John 8:34-36, Psalm 119:45, Deuteronomy 31:8*

MAY 31

Text: *Luke 5:8-9: Go away from me, Lord; I am a sinful man…. Don't be afraid; from now on you will catch men.*

Simon Peter stands in front of Jesus covered with shame and guilt and realizes how fallen he is in the presence of righteousness. And Jesus says to him, "Don't be afraid." Our guilt and our shame create in us a great fear, as God's holiness and goodness reveal our fallenness and our shame. Over and over in His word God speaks to us to tell us not to be afraid, for He will take that which causes our fear, our failings, and our sin, and He will allow us to be His disciples and follow Him. Guilt and shame do not have to be a permanent condition of our souls.

Will you give your fear to God?
Isaiah 43:1, Psalm 34:4-5, John 24:27, Romans 8:15

JUNE

JUNE 1

Text: *Acts 8:21: You have no part or share in their ministry, because your heart is not right before God.*

The Lord sent his Apostles and disciples out to minister to the world. In order to be sent, in order to be used, their hearts had to be "right," motivated by love for God, not by self-aggrandizement, greed, or lust for power over others. Their hearts were required to be hearts of servants and, if they were not, they could not be used in God's kingdom. Nothing has changed from that time to this. My heart cannot be right for ministering to others if the desires of my heart are the fleshly desires of the world.

> *What is your heart's desire?*
> *Matthew 7:22-23, Psalm 27:3, Matthew 23:28, Psalm 73:25-26*

JUNE 2

Text: *Acts 10:15: Do not call anything impure that God has made clean.*

All those that God has made clean are, in fact, clean. That includes me. I will not continue to call myself, or to think of myself, as impure, for God has cleansed me. I refuse to listen to the enemy when the enemy comes against me to convince me that I have not been cleansed. The enemy tells me that I have not been cleansed, and that the things that God declares to be impure are really pure. God's word does not change because Satan wants to convince me otherwise. What God has called sin, is sin, and His word cannot change--ever. I am clean because He has made me clean. Help me now, Lord, not to tarnish the cleansing work you have done in me.

> *Are you clean?*
> *1 John 1:9, Titus 2:12-14, Hebrews 9:14, Hebrews 10:22*

JUNE 3

Text: *Joshua 5:9: Today I have rolled away the reproach of Egypt from you.*

God had prepared His people to be whole. The cleansing took place with an entire generation perishing in the desert. Their leader, Moses, who was greatly loved by God, perished with them. God circumcised and healed a people, a new generation, preparing them for war. God stopped the waters of the Jordan so the new generation might enter His promised land, and after forty years they finally entered. The manna stopped. They became a whole people once more, ready to take that which God had given to them, that which God prepared for them. Lord, take from me, roll away from me, the reproach of my own personal Egypt. Make me whole. Give me the responsibility of taking the fruit of the land to which you have led me and bless me in the new generation, the regeneration of my soul.

Are you ready for God's abundance?
Romans 5:17, 2 Corinthians 9:8, Psalm 66:12, John 10:10

JUNE 4

Text: *2 Samuel 10:5: When David was told about this, he sent messengers to meet the men, for they were greatly humiliated.*

David's men had been shamed. Sent to offer comfort to one they believed to be a friend, they were instead met and humiliated by an enemy. David, in his godly wisdom, knows of their feelings of shame, and so instead of waiting for them to return in humiliation, he sends word to them to rest and heal. He does this to show them that they are still loved and cared for by their king. God has done this for me. David's men did nothing wrong, but I have sinned against God and covered myself with shame. But even in the midst of my sin and shame my King came to me to give me rest and healing, and to show that he loved me and cared for me. Thank you, my God and my King.

> *Will you accept God's rest?*
> *Matthew 11:28-30, Psalm 4:8, Hebrews 4:10-11, Isaiah 26:3*

JUNE 5

Text: *Ezra 9:15: Here we are before you in our guilt, though because of it not one of us can stand in your presence.*

Ezra learned of the people's sin and he was "appalled." He sat before God with his head bowed, unable to look up at God because he was so ashamed. He confessed to God on behalf of his people that after all that God had done for them, after all the mercy that God had shown to his people, they had deliberately disobeyed God's word. He acknowledged that they were worthy of being wiped from the face of the Earth, worthy of being wiped out completely. Lord, here I am before you in my guilt, and I am not able to stand in your presence. Make me to be appalled by my sin, and make me to hang my head in your presence. But you, my Lord, are the lifter of my head.

> *Are you ashamed?*
> *Romans 10:11, 1 John 2:28, 2 Corinthians 7:10, Romans 6:21*

JUNE 6

Text: *Job 11:14&15: If you put away the sin that is in your hand and allow no evil to dwell in your tent, then you will lift up your face without shame; and you will stand firm and without fear.*

The advice coming from Zophar to Job was perhaps misplaced. The advice coming from God's word to me certainly is not. God has forgiven me my sin, and I know that He has, but I fear the evil that I have allowed to remain. God has forgiven and will forgive me even of that, but it is my responsibility to cast out that which is not of God if I am to stand before my heavenly father. It is not about God's forgiveness, which is always there, but about my obedience, which is not as constant. God accepts me and loves me always, but the enemy brings sin to tempt me and, after I have looked upon sin, the shame is so great that I cannot stand before God. Lord, I must be cleansed, not for others, or even for myself, but for you and for the sake of your love for me.

Does sin remain in your life?
1 John 3:9, Romans 6:13-14, 2 Corinthians 13:5, Jeremiah 31:19

JUNE 7

Text: *Job 20:3: I hear a rebuke that dishonors me, and my understanding inspires me to reply.*

What is Zophar saying? Job's words offend Zophar? He knows better than Job because he is so wise? It is all about Zophar! His words are not meant to comfort Job but to vindicate Zophar. Here we have Job, sitting in a pile of ashes, his family killed, his treasure plundered and burned, and his body covered with sores that cause him great and constant pain, and Zophar's self-righteousness reveals that, "It's about me, Job, that's why I'm here." The world today does this to us, to those of us who hurt, who have fallen, those who are afflicted. The world comes not to comfort us, especially if we belong to God, but to share with us what our problem is. But after all, Jesus, this is really between you and me, and the voice of the world will not help. I must hear your voice only.

To whom are you listening?

John 10:27-28, Romans 10:17, Luke 11:18, Psalm 95:6-8

JUNE 8

Text: *Hosea 7:2: But they do not realize that I remember all their evil deeds. Their sins engulf them; they are always before me.*

Lord, every sin that I have committed clings to my soul like a stain, like blood that has dried on white linen. I am covered by the blood of my sin; the stains are so great that all anyone can see is the stain instead of my soul beneath. I am like a man covered with tattoos so that all you can see are the tattoos, not the man, as he hides beneath his ink, just as I hide beneath my sin. But, Jesus, as I come to you, your precious, spotless blood pours over me and completely removes the stain. It doesn't cover it up--it does away with it. Thank you, Jesus, for your cleansing. Help me to be careful now, to keep the fabric of my soul free from stain.

Are you trying to hide in sin?

Proverbs 28:13, Ezekiel 8:12, Hebrews 4:12-13, Psalm 10:11

JUNE 9

Text: *Zechariah 3:4: See, I have taken away your sin, and I will put rich garments on you.*

The picture is of an Old Testament priest standing before God in his filthy rags--in his sin. God strips him of his filthy clothing; he removes his sin, and he replaces the rags with rich, beautiful garments. God cannot put the new garments on the priest, over the rags, and the priest cannot take his filthy clothing, his sin, off of himself. God does it for him. God does the same thing for me. God does the same thing for you. Why, then, do I allow myself to be tempted to put my filthy rags back on over God's rich garments? Lord, help me to burn the old clothes.

What are you wearing?

1 John 3:4-9, 2 Corinthians 5:17, Luke 6:46, John 10:27-29

JUNE 10

Text: *Hebrews 8:12: For I will forgive their wickedness and will remember their sins no more.*

This is God's promise to us. Do you really believe it? Do I? Do I merely assent to the concept on an intellectual level, or do I cherish in my heart God's actual forgiveness? So many times I have allowed the enemy to re-insert my past sin into my present thoughts. The enemy's goal is to bring shame upon me, convincing me that I am not who God says I am. Satan would have me believe that I am a sinner, locked in my sin forever, instead of a forgiven sinner, whose sin has been wiped away by Jesus and who is a beloved child of God. Lord, I want to see myself as you see me: forgiven, clean, and your child.

Are you free of your past?

John 8:36, Galatians 5:1, Psalm 119:45, Romans 8:1-2

JUNE 11

Text: *Psalm 38:4: My guilt has overwhelmed me, like a burden too heavy to bear.*

My guilt and shame washed over me like a mudslide, and I was carried away in the midst of it. It was all I could think about as I walked daily with my head upon my chest, not daring to look at my fellow man, and certainly not able to reach for the hand of God. So, God reached for my hand instead and bathed me in his love and forgiveness. He lifted my head so that my eyes would be level with those of my brothers and sisters, so that I could look at the face of God. It is truly a miracle, Lord, that in my guilt and shame you loved me so much that you healed my sin, and guilt, and shame. As I walk with you, I will never be overwhelmed again.

> *Does your sin overwhelm you?*
> *Psalm 91:1-2, John 14:1, Psalm 94:19, Isaiah 40:31*

JUNE 12

Text: *Luke 1:25: "The Lord has done this for me," she said. "In these days he has shown his favor and taken away my disgrace among the people."*

Elizabeth's "disgrace" was that she had not borne a child. My disgrace is my sin. God took Elizabeth's disgrace from her by giving her a child. She had to wait, and she had to endure the scorn of others while she waited, but when God moved, in His time, He not only gave her a child but a child who would grow into one of God's mightiest men. God will heal my disgrace also, even though I am the one who invited it. It may take some time, for after all it is in his timing, not mine; but I know that my shame will be removed. God removed Elizabeth's disgrace publicly. God will take away my disgrace publicly. He will not allow me to hide behind silence and deceit. But rather by my telling what He has done for me, He will restore me.

Are you disgraced?

Psalm 44:15, Jeremiah 17:13, Psalm 119:39, Romans 10:9-11

JUNE 13

Text: *Isaiah 11:5: Righteousness will be his belt, and faithfulness the sash around his waist.*

This is a prophetic description of Jesus more than half a millennium before Jesus' birth. It is a description of who Jesus was to be. When Jesus called his disciples, He taught them to be like Him. When I accepted Jesus into my life, He called me to be like Him. My identity, then, must be as is His. I want this verse to describe me. I truly desire to be righteous before God. It is my great wish to be faithful and obedient to God, and to His word. I must be faithful to my wife and to those I love. I pray that these words describe who I am.

Will you walk in obedience?

John 15:14, Luke 11:28, Psalm 128:1, John 14:23

JUNE 14

Text: *Isaiah 62:12: They will be called the Holy people and the redeemed of the Lord.*

Who am I? Do I belong to the world, or am I really one of the Holy people? My sin belongs to the world, but I do not. I cast away my sin because it must be alien to me. I pray that I might be counted as one of the Holy people, the redeemed of the Lord. I am counted by God as such because of His redemption and the imputation of His holiness to me. I desire that this would be so obviously who I am, that not only would the Lord see me as such, but that the world might see me this way also. Lord, let me live your salvation boldly. Let me live it out loud.

Where do you belong?
Romans 8:9, 1 Peter 2:9, 1 Corinthians 6:19-20, Romans 8:38-39

JUNE 15

Text: *Luke 20:26: And astonished by his answer, they became silent.*

Jesus' answer was given to those who had come to Him to try and trick Him, to put Him in an impossible situation with an unanswerable question. The question was unanswerable only to them, not to Jesus. Today, Lord, today, you reveal truth to me. You speak to me in your word, your work, your still small voice, and in the crashing waves of dilemma. I talk too much, Lord. I need to become silent. I need to be astonished. I am not trying to trick you, Lord; I would not do such a thing. But that does not mean that I should not be amazed and fall silent before you.

Does God amaze you?
Psalm 40:5, Luke 9:43, Psalm 147:5, Matthew 8:26-27

JUNE 16

Text: *Genesis 1:26: Let us make man in our image.*

It was God. It was the Holy Spirit that moved over the waters; it was Jesus, the holy word. In unison you decided to make man, and to make him "in your image." I look like you, Lord. I don't know if I look like you on the outside, but I am created to look like you on the inside. Lord, when I die, this Earthly flesh will flee from my soul and my spirit will come home to you. I pray to you, Lord, that when that happens you will have made me and molded me and restored me to the point that my spirit looks like you, and that I may live forever, looking like you, as one of your children who has finally come home.

> *Who's your daddy?*
> *1 John 3:1, John 1:12-13, Matthew 23:9, Romans 8:16*

JUNE 17

Text: *1 Chronicles 7:40: All these were the sons of Asher, heads of the father's houses, choice and mighty men of valor, heads of the princes. (NASB)*

These were the descendants of Asher. They were men who were obedient to the authority over them. They were "heads of their father's houses." They did not rebel against their fathers, but rather took upon themselves the responsibilities assigned to them. They were "choice" men; men who would be chosen first if someone were choosing an elite band of men. They were "mighty men of valor," unafraid, intrepid warriors, not afraid to lead in battle, never sitting back and letting someone else take the risk. They were "heads of princes." Of all the mighty warriors in the army, these were the men that the troops would look up to and would choose to follow in battle. Lord, you have chosen me to be like them. Help me to be such a man.

> *Will you be God's obedient warrior?*
> *Jeremiah 29:11-12, 2 John v6, John 14:23, Psalm 119-57-61*

JUNE 18

Text: *Job 33:27: Then he comes to men and says, "I sinned and perverted what was right, but I did not get what I deserved."*

God knows me and knows that this passage describes my life accurately. I was deep in sin in my life, but God reached down and pulled me from the pit of destruction and cleansed me. He clothed me in his armor and made of me a warrior. God did not restore me to what I had been before the sin, but instead made me into what he intended for me all along. He guided me, and is guiding me, to my destiny. He is making me to be a warrior, the position he had chosen for me from the beginning of time. It is not what I deserve, and I am so grateful.

Will you get what you deserve?
Psalm 103:10-12, Romans 6:23, 1 John 1:9, Acts 22:16

JUNE 19

Text: *Matthew 16:15: "But what about you?" he asked, "Who do you say I am?"*

God asked this question of his disciples. He asks me the same question today. What I say when I answer is critical, but no less critical is the way in which I say it. Do I recite the fact that He is my savior, my Lord and my God, the son of the Living God, in the same way that I answer when someone asks for my telephone number? Do I answer God's question from my head or from my heart? I imagine Jesus standing in front of me, and as He gazes into my eyes, He holds me, captivates me, and asks me, "What about you, who do you say I am?" Could I possibly reply, "Sure, you're God," and keep on clicking through the TV channels? No, I would fall to my knees in worship of my Savior. You ask often, Lord, and I am afraid I give my answer carelessly, thoughtlessly. Lord, change that in me.

How do you answer God?
Isaiah 6:5, Exodus 3:4-6, James 4:10, 2 Samuel 7:18-22

JUNE 20

Text: *Mark 9:7: This is my son, whom I love. Listen to him!*

God settled, once and for all, any question about the identity of Jesus. Jesus is the Son of God. He is, therefore, not only my God, but also my brother, because I am the adopted son of God. I was not born as His child, for every man, save Jesus, has been born into a sinful world, and is separated from God by sin. But my brother, Jesus, my Lord, my Savior, has taken that sin and welcomed me into the family. God tells me to listen to Jesus, and Jesus speaks to me through the words of the Bible, and in those quiet moments when I listen for His voice. So often I talk instead of listening. Father, help me to listen for your words given to me by Jesus and the Holy Spirit.

> *Do you listen to God?*
> *Luke 11:28, Matthew 4:4, Revelation 3:20-22, John 10:27-28*

JUNE 21

Text: *Luke 10:49: But Martha was distracted with much serving.*

Martha was busy. In her own way she was serving the Lord. She had welcomed Him into her home, and she welcomed His guests and hers. She kept everything clean and neat and comfortable. She was very good at it. She had the gift of hospitality. She was selfless, serving others, loving other people and making sure that they were taken care of. This was service to others and is to be much admired. The problem was that her service to others became who she was, not what she did. The word says she was "distracted." She was distracted from sitting with God and listening to His voice; really finding out who He was and what His heart was. There is nothing

114

wrong with good works. In fact, God requires them of us; but we cannot become so overtaken by them that we don't have time for Jesus.

Does your service distract you?

Colossians 3:1-2, Mark 6:31, Psalm 46:10, Isaiah 26:31

JUNE 22

Text: *Ephesians 1:4: For he chose us in him before the creation of the world to be holy and blameless in his sight.*

God chose us. He reached down from heaven, pointed at you and me, and said, "This one." It was God's decision that we would be the ones in this world that would be holy and blameless, the ones that would honor Him and His decrees. But I have failed Him. I am not holy and blameless: I have sinned. Am I saying that God made a mistake when he chose me? Of course not. God is never wrong. So, what then, am I to think? God says that when I sin, and then repent and confess, he forgives me, and I am once more holy and blameless in His sight. It is not how the world sees me, or how I see myself. It is how God sees me. I am who He created me to be.

Are you who God created you to be?

1 Peter 2:9, Ephesians 1:11-12, Psalm 138:8, Proverbs 19:21

JUNE 23

Text: *Ephesians 4:1: As a prisoner for the Lord, then, I urge you to live a life worthy of the calling you have received.*

We have received a calling from the Lord. Our calling may not be to the pastorate, or to be a preacher, or to stand on a platform before thousands exhorting them to come to Jesus. Our calling may simply be to be a good dad, or a diligent workman in the marketplace, or a loving husband. But make no mistake: if we have received Christ as our savior, we have received a calling. But how can I fulfill my calling if I act unworthily? How can I be what God wants me to be if I continue to do all the evil and worldly things that I did before I came to Christ? I must be worthy of God's calling and His plan for me. And I can only be who He has called me to be because of His strength and mercy.

Will you receive God's calling?

2 Timothy 1:8-9, Romans 11:29, Galatians 5:13, 1 Peter 2:9

JUNE 24

Text: *Proverbs 7:26: Many are the victims she has brought down; her slain are a mighty throng.*

All of us think that we are special; I do. When the soft hand of temptation reaches out to me, I somehow believe that it reaches out only to me, because I am so special. Temptation deals in quantity. It cares not who I am, or who I think I am, as long as it can embrace me with evil. I am deluded into thinking that I am the only one. I am not; but when evil seduces me, she makes me believe I am. When sin has me firmly in her grasp and I struggle to break free and am unable to pull myself from the cesspool of sin, I look around and find that I am just another sinner, seduced by the evil one, and not special at all. My only avenue of escape is the realization that, after all, I am special in God's eyes, and because I am special to Him, He will pull me out of my sin.

Are you special to God?

Psalm 139:13-16, Luke 12:6-7, Isaiah 43:4, Deuteronomy 7:6

JUNE 25

Text: *Revelation 5:10: You have made them to be a kingdom and priests to serve our God and they will reign on the earth.*

About whom is this being said? It is said of the men and women that have been purchased by the blood of the Lamb. We are purchased for God's purpose, not our own. We are purchased to establish His kingdom on this Earth as His priests. We have been purchased to reign on the Earth, to control, to govern, to rule over all the Earth as priests of God's kingdom. But we must not mistakenly believe that we will reign over the Earth that now exists in the hands of the enemy. We will never govern the enemy's world. But we will reign in the spiritual world, today, here in this place. For today we are priests of God's spiritual world that exists even in the midst of the enemy camp. We must keep our priesthood pure. We must not let the enemy touch us.

> *Would you rule in the enemy's kingdom?*
> *1 John 5:19, John 16:11, Colossians 1:13-14, Ephesians 6:12*

JUNE 26

Text: *Jeremiah 30:17: But I will restore you to health and heal your wounds, declares the Lord ...*

Our God promises healing and restoration as we turn to Him and allow Him to touch us in the places that we have hidden. I have those places, places where no one can go but me; but if I turn to God, I will allow him to take me there. They are places, moments in time, events that have occurred in my life that are so painful that I don't want to revisit them, and I certainly don't want you to know anything about them. But once I say to

God, "All right, go ahead, you can take me back to any and every part of my life; I'll hold nothing back from you," then he begins to heal me. God's restoration is Him taking me back to the time when the world stole my identity through the lies of the enemy and through sin. God gives back to me the innocence that I never had. It is the restoring of the identity that God has for me because of His sacrifice.

What are you keeping from God?
Psalm 44:21, Psalm 90:8, Mark 4:22, Ephesians 5:11

JUNE 27

Text: *Luke 1:78: …because of the tender mercy of our God…*

These words are a part of the prophecy over John the Baptist. John's life was not an easy one. He lived in the desert without fine clothing, sumptuous food, or luxurious houses. He was a powerful spiritual force that so enraged the establishment that they imprisoned him and eventually beheaded him. But John was blessed in his relationship to Jesus and in his relationship to God. John never wavered or fled from his calling, and in the midst of all that happened to him, God's mercy was upon him that he might be blessed. Lord, your mercy is abundant, tender, and never harsh. It is the world that is harsh. You touch me with your gentle hand to reveal your plan for my life. Lord, let your plan be my plan. Let me no longer fear darkness and death, but let me live in your light, your salvation, your truth. Show me, oh Lord, your wonderful purpose for me.

How does God comfort you?
Psalm 23:4, John 14:16-17, Psalm 119-49-52, 2 Corinthians 1:3-4

JUNE 28

Text: *Luke 6:36: Be merciful just as your father is merciful.*

These are the words of Jesus teaching His disciples, teaching us how to treat our enemies. Lord, you know what I am going through right now, even with those that I love, with those to whom I have been close, those who now call me their enemy. I do not have it within me to be merciful right now. Deep within me I don't want mercy for them. I want justice--my justice. But you, Lord, tell me to be merciful, and I cannot do that of myself. I am only able to be merciful as you change me and change my heart. Lord, first change me, change my heart, and then use me to change my enemy by showing your mercy through me.

How do you treat your enemies?
Luke 6:27-31, Proverbs 24:17-18, Romans 12:19, 1 Peter 3:9

JUNE 29

Text: *Psalm 30:2: O Lord my God, I called to you for help and you healed me. O Lord, you brought me up from the grave, you spared me from going down into the pit.*

I had a disease, O Lord
Disobedience to you
The enemy had grown so strong
There was nothing I could do

I was slipping ever faster
Into the pit of Hell
And Satan thought he had me
Showed me where I would dwell

But you reached down into the pit
And took me by the hand
Brought me back from evil
To a place where I can stand

Only you could heal me, Lord
Save me from living death
You spared my life in mercy
I give you my dying breath

Is the enemy strong in your life?
Colossians 3:5-6, Psalm 19:13, James 4:7-8, Galatians 6:8

JUNE 30

Text: *Psalm 51:1: Have mercy on me, O God, according to your unfailing love; according to your great compassion blot out my transgressions.*

I do not deserve God's mercy. I stand before Him without excuse for my many sins. There were reasons that I engaged in sin, but there is no excuse. If I had an excuse, I could, perhaps, point to it to expiate myself. It is as if I stood accused of murder, and when I appeared before the Judge, I admitted that I had taken the life of another, but explained that the other person was such a terrible person and had hurt so many others that he had no right to live. The Judge would certainly reply that my explanation was not an excuse, but a reason, and that the law would consider my reason in mitigating my sentence but that my reason did not remove my guilt. So it is with my reasons for sin. They do not excuse me. The only hope that I have is God's mercy and unfailing love.

In His mercy, God has forgiven me.

What is your excuse?

John 15:22, Romans 1:20, Matthew 12:36, Romans 2:1

JULY

JULY 1

Text: *Isaiah 13:3: I have commanded my holy ones; I have summoned my warriors to carry out my wrath — those who rejoice in my triumph.*

God has made of me a warrior. I carry no sword but the sword of the Holy Spirit. I will take no life but my own, which I will surrender to my Lord. The war in which I fight is in the spiritual realm, and through the power of the Holy Spirit living in me I will conquer the evil that resides in sin rather than denizens of cities on foreign shores. But I am nonetheless a warrior, for God has called me to this fight.

> *Are you a warrior?*
> *Psalm 18:32, 1 Corinthians 16:13-14, Psalm 144:1-2, Joshua 1:9*

JULY 2

Text: *John 1:33: ...the man on whom you see the Spirit come down and remain is he who will baptize with the Holy Spirit.*

Jesus, in his mercy and grace, came to this Earth and was baptized. As He was baptized, the Holy Spirit, in all of his fullness, came upon Him and never left. Lord Jesus, I need that same touch of your Holy Spirit. I need for your Holy Spirit to remain, and I know that the Holy Spirit will remain as long as I do not drive Him away. I know that I really have no right to ask for the indwelling of the Spirit in my life, but Lord, I desire to follow you in the fullness of the Spirit, and so I do ask that you fill me now with your Holy Spirit.

> *Do you want the Holy Spirit in your life?*
> *Romans 8:10-11, Acts 1:4-5, John 16:13-15, John 14:16-18*

JULY 3

Text: *Acts 1:8: But you will receive power when the Holy Spirit comes on you, ...*

Lord, I desire to be filled more and more often with the power of the Holy Spirit. I know, Lord, that my flesh thirsts for power and acclamation but, Father, I rebuke that thirst in my flesh that would in any way glorify me. I ask for power, supernatural power, that will glorify you, not me or my flesh. I seek the power to accomplish your purpose in my life and in the lives of others. I want to be a part of healings, salvations and mercies that you ordain and that glorify you alone. Help me, Lord, to do your will.

> *Why do you want power?*
> *Proverbs 19:21, James 3:14-16, Acts 8:19, Romans 8:26*

JULY 4

Text: *2 Kings 9:22: "How can there be peace" Jehu replied, "as long as all the idolatry and witchcraft of your mother Jezebel abound?"*

Sin destroys peace. God has chosen peace for me and for my family. He has chosen a godly way of life; He has chosen obedience. He has chosen security and freedom from the strife of the world, so that we may live at peace with Him. Sin is my enemy. When I allow sin into my life, even a little sin, the war begins between the Holy Spirit of God that dwells in me and the sin, and there is no peace in my life because I have become the battleground. Lord, help me to be pure, to stop the war, to have peace.

> *Do you have peace?*
> *1 Peter 3:11, Psalm 85:8, Philippians 4:6-7, Isaiah 55:12*

JULY 5

Text: *1 Chronicles 20:1: In the spring, at the time when kings go off to war,*

What is it, Lord, about man that when the Earth comes alive again, and all of life begins to flow with new sap and new wine, that at this time man goes out to battle? Is it the lure of treasure and conquest? Is it the competition? Why, in this season, when your world--the world you created is so beautiful and green--do men go out to cover the Earth with blood? Perhaps, Lord, it is the renewed vigor in a man that gives him the energy and the arrogance to take things by force. Lord, I ask that not only in the spring, but all year long, you would renew my vigor in the spiritual war I fight. Renew my strength, Father, for constant and eternal conquest of my spiritual enemy.

> *What is your war?*
> *2 Corinthians 10:3-5, 1 Timothy 6:11-12, 1 John 5:3-5, 1 Corinthians 15:57-58*

JULY 6

Text: *Ezekiel 1:12: Each one went straight ahead. Where-ever the Spirit would go, they would go, without turning as they went.*

The creatures in Ezekiel's dream followed God's Holy Spirit. They did not try to control its movement; they did not resist its movement; they did not try to get ahead of the Spirit or outrace it. The creatures simply followed the Spirit, going wherever the Spirit went without any turning. You have called me to be like one of the creatures. I must follow the Holy Spirit; I must go where it takes me, without turning, without trying to get ahead of the Holy Spirit, never trying to control it, but rather being totally obedient to the Spirit's guidance and direction. I will move ahead boldly, without fear.

Do you obey the Holy Spirit?
Romans 8:13-14, John 14:26, Galatians 5:25, Psalm 143:9-10

JULY 7

Text: *Nahum 1:8: ...he will pursue his foes into darkness.*

G od's word teaches us to fight offensively as well as defensively. God's enemy, and mine, lives in dark places. They are the dark places of the world, the cesspools of evil that only the mind of man could invent, the dark places of my soul. But God commands us not only to protect ourselves from the evil one but to come against him. In the battle that is being waged even now, I am to go, at the side of my Lord, against the enemy, and to pursue him into the darkness where he lives and to destroy him in the darkness of the world and the darkness of my mind and soul.

Will you fight the enemy?
Ephesians 6:11, 1 Timothy 6:12, Psalm 44:5-7, Psalm 18:39

JULY 8

Text: *Malachi 2:16: So take heed to your spirit that you do not deal treacherously. (NASB)*

G od's word says that if I have the least bit of the Holy Spirit within me, I will not deal treacherously with man or with God. I must take heed of the Holy Spirit within me; I must pay attention to the Holy Spirit. I must tend the Holy Spirit within that I may never ignore Him, and walk away from Him, thus being left to my own devices and the belief that treachery is good and profitable. God's word says to me that job number one for me is to concentrate on the Holy Spirit within me that I may rely on God, not on myself.

Do you heed the Holy Spirit?
Romans 8:13-14, Ephesians 4:30, 1 Corinthians 3:16, Acts 5:3

JULY 9

Text: *Romans 7:22-23: For in my inner being I delight in God's law; but I see another law at work in my body…*

In my inner being, in the person that I really am, in my soul and my desire for intimacy with God, I long for obedience and purity before God. But my body betrays me. It sends signals to my mind and my heart, tempting me to satisfy the lust of the flesh. The rewards that my body offers to me are fleeting and temporal, while the rewards of obedience are eternal. The rewards of the flesh are shame and isolation, while the rewards of obedience are communion with the living God and peace. How can I defeat the body and dwell in the spirit? I cannot in my own strength, but the Holy Spirit can and will lead me there.

Do you live in the flesh or the Spirit?
Galatians 5:16, Romans 8:10, Matthew 26:41, Ephesians 2:3-5

JULY 10

Text: *1 Timothy 6:12: Fight the good fight of the faith.*

I am in a battle, and I will continue to be in a battle as long as I live in this world. Like the wars I see unfolding in the world around me, the battles will ebb and flow. There will be moments of peace in the midst of war, hours of calm, days of joy, but the battle remains. The war is the conflict between my spirit that I have surrendered to God and my flesh that remains in the world. Each day I must deal with the demands that my flesh places upon me. God has not called me to live a life of peace but a life of war. He has not called me to be passive but to be aggressive. He has not called me to lay down my arms but to take them up. God has not called me to an easy life, but he has called me to a victorious life.

> *Are you at war?*
>
> *Ephesians 6:12, 1 Peter 5:8, Psalm 144:1, Romans 7:21-23*

JULY 11

Text: *2 Timothy 1:14: Guard the good deposit that was entrusted to you – guard it with the help of the Holy Spirit who lives in us.*

The good deposit that was entrusted to me is the knowledge of, and fellowship with, Christ, my God and King and Father. I must guard it closely because the enemy constantly seeks to rob me of this great gift by his deception and attack. But I have been given also, along with the gift, the power of the Holy Spirit to keep it safe from the enemy. If a home, and all that is in it, is protected by an alarm, the alarm does no good until it is turned on. So, too, although I have the Holy Spirit, I must activate him in my life by invitation, by prayer, and by surrender. Come now, Holy Spirit, and guard the precious gift within me.

> *Is the Holy Spirit at work in you?*
>
> *Romans 15:13, Romans 5:5, 2 Corinthians 3:17, Galatians 5:22-23*

JULY 12

Text: *Psalm 104:30: When you send your spirit, they are created, and you renew the face of the earth.*

Your spirit comes
The Earth lives
You fall on man
And man is

Creation of old
Has come from you
You do with us
As you choose to do

Come again
Fall anew
Revive the world
Not just a few

Give new breath
Give new life
Come Holy Spirit
Recreate life

Are you alive in the Holy Spirit?
John 3:5-6, John 6:63, Galatians 6:8, Isaiah 44:3-4

JULY 13

Text: *Acts 1:6: When they heard this sound, a crowd came together in bewilderment, because each one heard them speaking in his own language.*

The Apostles and the crowd saw signs and wonders; they heard the sound of a roaring wind and observed what appeared to be tongues of fire. It is interesting to note that there was no roaring wind, which would have caused great loss and probably injury; nor were there tongues of fire, which would probably have ignited a conflagration which would have created a stampede among the people. It was, instead, the sound and appearance of these things that they experienced. It got the disciples' attention, and it got the attention of a great crowd of people. The crowd heard the Apostles speaking in their own languages. The Apostles, however, were not speaking in other known languages but in the tongues given to them by the Holy Spirit, and the Holy Spirit used the language to speak to the crowds. As the Holy Spirit speaks today, no matter what language or kind of communication He chooses to use, I must open my ears to hear.

Will you listen to the Holy Spirit?
John 14:26, Hebrews 3:15, John 16:13, Galatians 3:5

JULY 14

Text: *Acts 4:31: After they prayed, the place where they were meeting was shaken. And they were all filled with the Holy Spirit and spoke the word of God boldly.*

I say that I want the experience of being filled with the Holy Spirit. Do I really? Why is it that I want to be filled with the Holy Spirit? Just for the feeling, the rush, the signs and wonders that will amaze me? The Holy Spirit will not fall upon me for the purpose of titillation. He comes to do God's work through me, if I allow him to do so. In this passage, Peter had just spoken truth in a very hostile environment and Jesus' followers prayed to be filled with the Holy Spirit power that they had just seen in Peter. Then they all "spoke the word of God boldly." Do I want the Holy Spirit power so that I will speak God's word boldly? Is it my desire to convict, to touch, to heal others in God's power, or do I just want to play games?

Why do you want to be filled with the Holy Spirit?

1 Corinthians 12:7, Romans 8:26-27, 1 Corinthians 2:10-16, Galatians 5:22-23

JULY 15

Text: *John 13:23: One of them, the disciple whom Jesus loved, was reclining next to him.*

Lord, I don't want to be like the disciple that you love; I want to *be* the disciple you love. A bold request? Yes! But you know, Lord, that what I am really asking is that you show me how to be the disciple that you love, not that you would extend your love to me in any fuller measure than you already have. Lord, it is what I do with your love, the love that you have for me right now, that determines my relationship to you. Lord, show me what I must do to lay hold of that love. Show me how to be the disciple that you love.

Is God's love personal for you?

Romans 5:8, John 5:13, Isaiah 54:10, Psalm 27:4

JULY 16

Text: *John 13:34: A new command I give you: Love one another. As I have loved you, so you must love one another. By this all men will know that you are my disciples, if you love one another.*

Lord, if I am to "love one another" in the way that you love me, I must first know your love. I cannot settle for understanding your love for me intellectually, or even giving assent to the fact that you love me. I must experience your love, for only then will I know your love. Only to the extent that I experience your love am I able to keep your command to love others. When

I do experience your love, I cannot keep myself from sharing it with others. When I do not experience your love, I have nothing within me with which to love anyone else.

Do you experience God's love?

Ephesians 3:17-19, Romans 5:5, 1 John 3:1, Psalm 13:5-6

JULY 17

Text: *John 20:18: Mary Magdalene went to the disciples with the news: "I have seen the Lord!"*

Mary Magdalene, a former demoniac who had been delivered by Jesus, was the first to see Him. Why her? Was it because the Lord loved her? Was it because she was so devoted to Jesus and loved Him so much? Was it because she had been healed and delivered by Him? Of course, the answer to all of these questions is yes, but for me another reason is very important. She was at the grave and would not stop looking for Him. Jesus, you have delivered me also, and I am so grateful. Help me Lord, to never stop seeking you and your presence.

Are you looking for God?

Jeremiah 29:13, Psalm 63:1, 2 Chronicles 7:14, Matthew 7:7

JULY 18

Text: *John 21:19: Jesus said this to indicate the kind of death by which Peter would glorify God. Then he said to him "Follow me!"*

Jesus has just told Peter what the cost would be for Peter to follow him. But Jesus didn't ask Peter to follow him--he asked Peter if he loved him. When Peter confirmed, for himself, that he did indeed love Jesus, then the

Lord commanded Peter to follow Him. The question has never been if I would follow my Lord; the question is do I love Him? If I truly love Him, the command to follow Him is for my benefit, my protection. If I truly love my Lord, I must follow Him, because that is where the protection and the blessings lie.

Will you follow the Lord?
John 8:12, Mark 8:34-35, Joshua 24:15, 1 Peter 2:21

JULY 19

Text: *Song of Solomon 1:4: Take me away with you—let us hurry! Let the king bring me into his chambers.*

Lord, you are my love and I do love you. If you choose to take me away, let it be so. Hide me away in your private places, Lord, just us. I can hardly believe that the mightiest one of the universe loves me and seeks to steal away alone with me. Help me, Lord, to believe, and to experience that relationship to you, as I come to you in the quiet times, when you and I are alone together.

Are you ever alone with God?
Matthew 6:6, Matthew 14:23, James 4:8, Psalm 46:10

JULY 20

Text: *Song of Solomon 3:2: …I will search for the one that my heart loves.*

My heart does love you, Lord, and I search for you. But I must search in the right places. I will not find you in the city nor in the throngs of people, even though you are there, I know. I will not find you in the shops or the places that tempt my eye. I will find you, oh Lord, in the quiet times of dawn when I awake and seek you and find you seeking me.

Where do you find God?
Acts 17:27-28, Jeremiah 29:13, Proverbs 8:17, Psalm 105:3-4

JULY 21

Text: *Song of Solomon 5:3: I have taken off my robe – must I put it on again? I have washed my feet – must I soil them again?*

Lord, you have come to me over and over again in my lifetime. You have prepared yourself to live in intimacy with me, but I would not allow you to enter into the private places where I lived. I ignored your presence and closed the door of my chambers, my private abode. I sent you away, forcing you to again don the clothing that you had shed to reveal yourself to me. Lord, I have opened the doorway, and I lie on the bed of my life, open and vulnerable to you. I await your arrival and your perfect touch upon my soul.

Do you welcome God's touch?
Mark 1:40-42, Luke 6:19, Matthew 17:5-8, Luke 15:20

JULY 22

Text: *Song of Solomon 7:6: How beautiful you are and how pleasing, O love, with your delights!*

In this verse and in the entire chapter, God speaks to me of my body that he created for his good pleasure. It speaks to me of the beauty of my sexuality, created for God's pleasure and mine. It tells me that God is delighted in my sexual relations, but only as I first surrender my sexuality to

Him and then enter into my marriage bed as He designed it and intended it. Lord, I love you, and I surrender my physical body, as well as my sexuality, to you. Come, Lord, and touch me as you wish this day. Bring me delight, Father, and let me delight you.

> *Have you surrendered your desires to God?*
> *Ephesians 5:25-27, 1 Corinthians 6:17, Galatians 5:16, Psalm 37:4*

JULY 23

Text: *Song of Solomon 8:10: …Thus I have become in his eyes like one bringing contentment.*

Lord, I pray that you will look upon me and that I will bring contentment to you rather than strife or sorrow. I pray that my life, my marriage, my walk with you, my family, will bring contentment to you. Help me, Lord, to be content with your love for me and not seek after some lesser pleasure. Lord, I surrender my spiritual virginity to you. I have never given myself totally to anyone or anything; but today I surrender totally to you and, having done so, I also surrender to my wife. As you love me, I love her. Lord, that you may be content with me, and that I may be content with her.

> *Are you content?*
> *1 Timothy 6:6, Philippians 4:12-13, Matthew 6:25-26, Psalm 23*

JULY 24

Text: *Luke 5:16: But Jesus often withdrew to lonely places and prayed.*

Jesus did not go to the busy places, crowded with good acts, to pray. He did not go to places crowded with people, nor to the holy places, churches, or synagogues. He did not go to the places that were crowded with people doing good deeds, and not even to the places where his disciples gathered. Jesus went to lonely places. Just Jesus and the Father, and no one else, was where he found comfort, solace and communion. It was where the only voice that spoke to him was the voice of his Father and the cacophony of the world didn't drown out the Father's voice. God's thoughts were not snatched from his mind. A lonely place is a good place, the best place; for it is there I will not be alone.

Do you go to lonely places?
Matthew 6:6, Mark 1:35, Psalm 62:1, Psalm 32:7

JULY 25

Text: *Luke 8:21: He replied, "My mother and brothers are those who hear God's word and put it into practice."*

Lord, I so desire to truly be in your family. I desire to be your son, your brother. I am related to you by blood, your blood that cleansed me from my sin and brought me salvation. Father, let me; help me to start acting like a member of your family. I must hear your word, and I must do your word. Lord, let me not be estranged from your family because I have left the family to live in the world. I want to come home, Lord; I want to live in your family--with you.

Do you live in God's family?
1 John 3:1, Ephesians 2:19, Acts 17:28, Romans 8:16

JULY 26

Text: *Luke 9:3: He told them: "Take nothing for the journey – no staff, no bag, no bread, no money, no extra tunic."*

Lord, you have sent me to touch your people, and I am to leave all of me behind. I am not to take any of my own talents, wealth, position, or family background. I must leave my pride, theology, church membership or anything else that I believe makes me who I am or makes me important. For as I take anything with me, I diminish the room within me that is to be filled with the Holy Spirit. And I know that your Holy Spirit is the only thing that touches the heart of your creation.

What do you need to touch others?
2 Timothy 3:16-17, John 1:23, Hebrews 13:20-21, Ephesians 6:10

JULY 27

Text: *Genesis 20:15: My land is before you; live wherever you like.*

It is hard for me to understand with my limited human understanding: Abraham and Sarah lied to Abimelech, and Abimelech did not knowingly sin against God, or against Abraham and Sarah, in his relationship to them. Yet, in spite of this, Abimelech makes restitution to Abraham and Sarah and they profit. It is, I suppose, that God protected Abraham and Sarah, not because of their sin, but in spite of the sin. God must have loved them so much, and had his hand of protection on them so closely, that he blessed them in spite of what they had done in not trusting God. Oh Lord, that you would love me that much. But, in fact, you do. Have you not blessed me in spite of my sin? Surely, then, I have seen your love for me.

Is your blessing undeserved?
Hebrews 4:16, Psalm 103:10, 2 Timothy 1:8-9, 2 Corinthians 12:9

JULY 28

Text: *Genesis 33:10: If I have found favor in your eyes, accept this gift from me.*

It was a gift from Jacob to Esau. It is part of a biblical lesson. But, Lord, the words are also an example for me. If I have found favor with you, and I believe that I have, what gift would you have from me? I know that you don't desire or need my gift, but Lord, the giving of a gift is something I need to do for myself. What, though, could I possibly give to you? You already own the cattle on a thousand hills; you have the loyalty of those who are far greater than I. I try to give you my obedience, but so often I fail. All I have to give is the love of a broken and humbled man, disgraced by sin, and with few years left to serve you. But, what I have, Lord, I give to you. I give all of my love to you.

> *What will you give to God?*
> *Psalm 116:12-14, Mark 12:17, Matthew 25:40, Romans 12:1*

JULY 29

Text: *Exodus 26:33: The curtain will separate the Holy Place from the Most Holy Place.*

Many still live with the partition in place, in spite of the fact that Jesus' death on the cross removed the barrier between man and God. I must understand and experience the very real presence of God in my life, and not be content to remain in the "Holy Place" instead of being in the "Most Holy Place." Just as your people during the Exodus were content to remain in the desert, and not enter into the promise you had made to them, so I am tempted to remain in the church, and the safe place of a sanctuary crafted by man, and never enter into the relationship that you have crafted for me.

Thank you for calling me, Lord, and I will enter into the Most Holy Place, the place where you dwell.

Would you be closer to God?

1 Chronicles 16:11, Jeremiah 29:13, Proverbs 8:17, Psalm 27:8

JULY 30

Text: *Leviticus 16:2: Tell your brother Aaron not to come whenever he chooses into the Most Holy Place....*

Apparently, Aaron had begun to take his entry into the Most Holy Place for granted, not preparing, not cleansing, but rather simply coming and going as he pleased. God warns him not to do that, and in so doing warns me today. Do I seek to come into the presence of God lightly? I know that God loves me, and that I can come to Him at any time, but I must always remember that entering into the presence of God is not like walking into my favorite restaurant. I am welcome to go to God, and invite His presence, but God is not at my beck and call. I must be careful to come to God in a spirit of reverence and awe, and I will be welcomed as His child.

How do you approach God?

Hebrews 10:19-22. Psalm 24:3-4, Micah 6:8, Luke 18:10-12

JULY 31

Text: *Numbers 30:2: When a man makes a vow to the Lord or takes an oath to obligate himself by a pledge, he must not break his word but must do everything he said.*

L ord, I know that I have made vows that I have not honored. Show me Lord, remind me of all that I have said, and help me to keep all my vows. If I have made vows that were of my flesh, and evil in your sight, I ask forgiveness for having done so, and ask that you will excuse me from those vows, that I may not offend you. On my wedding day, I made a vow to you God, and to my wife. I have in the past violated that vow by the sin in my life. Lord, will you remind me of that vow each and every day, that I might honor you, and honor my wife in keeping the vow that I made?

Do your vows honor God?

Deuteronomy 23:21, Psalm 50:14, Psalm 61:8, Ecclesiastes 5:4-6

AUGUST

AUGUST 1

Text: *Deuteronomy 12:4: You must not worship the Lord in their way.*

I am tempted to worship the Lord as I see others worship Him, to conform to the world, to do what the Church is doing. When I worship in that way my expectations are that God will meet me and respond to me, as I perceive He is responding to others. It should not be. It is like seeing the interaction between two of my friends and desiring the same kind of relationship between myself and my friends that exists between them. So, I try to act like my friends and do the things they do so that I can have the same relationship as they have. In the process I have lost the true relationship that I could, and should, have with them. Lord, help me to be myself. Help me to have a relationship to you that is ours. Help me not to worship you in the way that anyone else does. Lord, I want our relationship to be real and to be authentic.

> *Is your relationship to God authentic?*
>
> *Acts 8:11-13, Psalm 118:8, 2 Timothy 4:3-5, 1 Corinthians 2:2-5*

AUGUST 2

Text: *1 Samuel 6:20: Who can stand in the presence of the Lord, this holy God?*

God did not come to satisfy my curiosity, nor to do my will. He didn't come to bring me pleasure and give me gifts of ease and comfort. He came as the mighty creator of all that is. How then, shall I, as His child who understands and has seen His holiness and might, try to stand before Him? I am not worthy to crawl into His presence or to even come near the place where He dwells. Instead, He comes to me in the place where I dwell to love me and comfort me, to fill me with His power and might, that I may truly serve Him in His power.

Will you accept God's mercy?

Matthew 9:13, Psalm 145:8-9, Psalm 107:13-16, Luke 19:10

AUGUST 3

Text: *2 Samuel 19:43: We have ten shares in the king, and besides, we have a greater claim on David than you have.*

Everybody loves a winner! These same people, who are now fighting over who is closer to King David, have just come through a time when the people had united against David and chosen the rebellious son, Absalom, as their leader. But Absalom has died. David reigns once more, and the people are pushing and shoving to get close to him. Mankind is so fickle; we know nothing of real loyalty except what we see in God. Jesus has shown us what it was like to love unconditionally and to be faithful. Lord, let me never love you for my own selfish reasons. Let me love you always because you are God.

Why do you love God?

1 John 4:19, Deuteronomy 30:16, Psalm 37:4-6, John 14:23-24

AUGUST 4

Text: *Hosea 2:16: In that day, declares the Lord, You will call me "my husband;" you will no longer call me "my master."*

Lord, our relationship is truly one of master and servant, for you are my king. But Lord, you are a benevolent king, and it is your desire that our relationship be much more than that of master and servant. If you are to me only a distant figure who hands out difficult tasks and sets rules and regulations for me to follow, then your love is lost on me, and I will surely stray from our relationship. But, if I know you, and if I love you and come to you each day as the love of my life, how could I ever abandon you?

Do you only fear God?
1 John 4:18, Psalm 34:4, Isaiah 41:10, Psalm 115:11

AUGUST 5

Text: *1 Corinthians 13:12: Now I know in part; then I shall know fully, even as I am fully known.*

Someday I will know fully. I will love fully. I will have no doubts, no questions, no fears. I will know completely and experience fully God's love for me. But even now, God knows me fully; even now I am known by Him in the fullness of His love. Someday I will enter into that love fully. I don't understand how that works; I just know this is what God has promised me. It seems that all my life I have been striving to be fully loved. Someday I will comprehend that all my life I have been fully loved.

How does God love you?
1 John 3:1, John 15:13, Zephaniah 3:17, Psalm 86:5

AUGUST 6

Text: *Ephesians 3:12: In him and through faith in him we may approach God with freedom and confidence.*

How do I approach my heavenly Father? As I was growing up, God was the King on the throne who could not be approached. It was unthinkable. For years, even after I had accepted the great gift of salvation, I felt I could only approach God in great fear. Knowing who I was and what I had done, I would also approach not daring to look at my Lord because I was not worthy to even raise my head. To some degree, all of these attitudes are right, but God has set them all to the side for me. He has reached out and touched me and said come, you may approach freely, any time you wish, and with confidence that I will always greet you with a smile.

How do you approach God?

Psalm 4:23-24, Hebrews 4:16, Matthew 27:51, Ephesians 2:13

AUGUST 7

Text: *Psalm 147:11: The Lord delights in those who fear him, who put their hope in his unfailing love.*

I am not afraid of you, Lord, but I fear you. My fear is born not in cowardice but in the realization of who you are. My fear is a kind of respect, or my respect is a kind of fear. You, Lord, are truly awesome, and I am filled with awe. There are no limits to your understanding; for after all, everything that has been created was created by you. The most intelligent of human beings can, perhaps, envision consequences of actions to the fourteenth or possibly the fifteenth consequence. You know with certainty the consequences of acts to the end of time. And yet, with all your power and all your might, still, you love me. I don't understand it, but I am grateful and I am filled with the wonder of you.

Do you fear God?

Psalm 19:9, Psalm 25:14, Proverbs 19:23, Isaiah 33:5-6

AUGUST 8

Text: *Psalm 145:16: You open your hand and satisfy the desires of every living thing.*

You invite me to come, much as a man holds out an apple to a wild deer. First the deer studies the man, wanting the apple, but afraid that the man will harm him. But the man moves not, and each day the deer becomes a little bolder, and draws a bit nearer, until finally the day comes when the deer snatches the apple from the man's hand and scampers off with its treasure. But the next day the deer returns and finds the man still there with another apple. And, so it goes, until one day the man reaches out to pet the deer, and the deer eventually allows the man's touch upon him and finds that it is good to be petted by the man. Eventually the deer lives in the presence of the man because the deer has come to love the man, not just the apple. I am that deer, Lord, and you are the man. I love *you*, not just your gifts.

> *Do you love God or just His gifts?*
> *1 John 2:16, Matthew 6:24, James 3:14-15, 2 Timothy 3:2-4*

AUGUST 9

Text: *Psalm 131:2: But I have stilled and quieted my soul, like a weaned child with its mother, like a weaned child is my soul within me.*

I truly desire to come to my Lord as a small child, weaned and no longer demanding to be fed, content to be in its mother's presence. The child desires only that the mother take it in her arms and hold it, that the child may again know the smell, the touch, the embrace of the mother and hear its mother's voice speak words of love. Lord, teach me how to do that. I have learned to walk, to fight, to contend. I have learned self-sufficiency and come to you as an adult, or perhaps as a rebellious teen, always asking for something, always desiring something, always worrying. Lord show me this day how to come to you and rest, to be content with your touch, your smell, your voice as you tell me gently how much you love me. Let me not seek any favor or blessing other than the very presence of you.

Will you rest in God's presence?

Psalm91:1, Matthew 11:28-29, Psalm 62:5, Psalm 4:8

AUGUST 10

Text: *Luke 14:24: For I tell you none of those men who were invited shall taste of my dinner. (NASB)*

Those who were invited were not enemies of the man giving the dinner; neither were they strangers. They were the man's friends. But they were all too busy with their own lives to take the time to fellowship with the one who extended the invitation. Am I not like that with God? Every morning God extends His hand to me and says, "Come, walk with me today," and every morning I say, "Please excuse me, God, but my day is already filled with plans." During the day he calls out to me, but I don't hear him because I am busy in conversation with others and concentrating on the tasks at hand. Before I sleep at the end of my day, I take the time to say goodnight and thanks to my God who has yearned all day to be with me. Will I then be present at the wedding banquet when Jesus returns, or will it already be filled with those who took the time to be God's friend?

Are you too busy for God?

Luke 10:38-42, 1 John 2:17, Psalm 37:7, Matthew 16:19-21

AUGUST 11

Text: *Acts 12:7: He struck Peter on the side and woke him up.*

Here's Peter, lying chained to two guards in a prison cell, with two more guards standing guard over the guards. Herod is going to bring Peter to trial the next morning, and he will then be executed as was his fellow Apostle James several days earlier. And yet, Peter sleeps. The angel has to wake him up in order to save him. How could he sleep? The world's answer would probably be that he was just so exhausted from the fear that must have gripped him that he could not stay awake. Perhaps. Much more likely, however, he sleeps because he is at peace with whatever his fate is to be. He walked with Jesus, he had committed his life into Jesus' hands, he had become a true apostle, accepting whatever life dealt him, because of his relationship to Jesus. Peter didn't look to Jesus only for salvation, for healing, for rescue; he also looked to Jesus as his friend and companion in whatever life held. Lord, that I might have that kind of faith and trust.

Will you trust God in spite of the circumstances?
Psalm 9:10, Joshua 1:9, Isaiah 41:10, Hebrews 13:6

AUGUST 12

Text: *1 Peter 3:7: Husbands, in the same way be considerate as you live with your wives, and treat them with respect as the weaker partner and as heirs with you of the gracious gift of life, so that nothing will hinder your prayers.*

Too often I allow myself to think of my spouse as a separate entity before God. She has her walk, and I have mine, and I need not concern myself too much for her as God will surely take care of her. When that happens, I abdicate my role as the leader of my family, as the spiritual head of my wife.

It is my duty to honor, to serve, to protect, and to lead my wife; for I am the head of our relationship and the protector of our marriage. Lord, help me to assume my responsibility each and every day and to be the husband that you have designed me to be.

Do you take spiritual responsibility in your family?
Ephesians 5:25, 1 Peter 3:7, Colossians 3:19, Ephesians 5:28

AUGUST 13

Text: *Ephesians 5:28: So husbands ought to love their own wives as their own bodies. (NASB)*

For many years I did love my wife as I loved my own body--and it was wrong. I loved my wife without respect, without care and concern, without thinking of anything but my own pleasure. I first had to learn to love my own body, to care for and nurture my own body, before I could truly care for my wife. I had to stop rushing off to experience every pleasure that the enemy offered to me. If I follow my carnal desires without regard to God's law, which is designed to protect me, I will ultimately die a wasted body in a corrupt world. So, too, if I love my wife in this selfish way, our love will die also. I must honor my body and honor my wife.

Are you a selfish spouse?
Ephesians 5:33, Genesis 2:24, 1 Corinthians 13:4-7, Ephesians 4:2

AUGUST 14

Text: *1 Timothy 2:14: And Adam was not the one deceived, it was the woman who was deceived and became a sinner.*

At first blush this seems an odd statement, that Eve was deceived, but Adam sinned knowingly, and that this somehow qualified him to lead. There is no natural intellectual superiority in men, so why should women not lead their husbands? I believe, though, that Paul is saying that the first sin was committed by Adam when he failed to lead. He abdicated the position that God had given him, along with his responsibility to Eve. Adam's knowledge did not qualify him to lead. God qualified him to lead, and he sinned when he knowingly ceded that leadership to Eve. Satan is still using the same tactic in the lives of men and women today. I must be aware of this danger.

Do you lead or are you led?
Genesis 3:17, 1 Peter 3:7, Ephesians 5:25-27, Colossians 3:19

AUGUST 15

Text: *Proverbs 31:30: Charm is deceitful and beauty is vain, but a woman who fears the Lord, she shall be praised.*

Do I become dissatisfied with the wife of my youth when I see young women in the marketplace and on the street? Their forms are attractive and sin tempts me to consider what a night with such a woman would be. But I must consider: would I really trade my wife for one of those? My wife is the one who has loved me all these years, tended to our children, provided a home and watched over me. She is the one in whom I have invested my life. Would I really be willing to give her up? For I can be assured that when I look upon another with desire, I have already taken the first step toward the death of our relationship, and Satan is right there to guide me the rest of the way. I do love my wife, and I must keep my thoughts and my eyes for her alone.

Are you faithful to your spouse?

Hebrews 13:4, Proverbs 5:18-19, 1 Corinthians 4:7, Matthew 19:9

AUGUST 16

Text: *Proverbs 30:21 & 23: Under three things the earth trembles, under four it cannot bear up… an unloved woman who is married.*

I am no longer going to fool myself. The continued use of pornography, masturbation, unfaithfulness to my wife in these things, prevents me from loving my wife as God intended. It is only when I have discarded the sin that I am able to see my wife for the gift that she truly is. It is only then that I will want to see her for the gift that she is to me. The world tells me, "It's my wife's fault that I am this way. She doesn't meet my sexual needs or desires." God says that I am the problem, not her. I am the leader of my home, and I must lead in purity and holiness. My wife does meet all my needs, but she is not to meet desires created by Satan in my sexual sin.

Do you trade love for lust?

Matthew 5:27-28, James 1:13-15, 1 Thessalonians 4:3-5, Proverbs 6:25-29

AUGUST 17

Text: *Isaiah 43:10: "You are my witnesses," declares the Lord "and my servant whom I have chosen."*

I am your servant, oh Lord, and I will testify to the wondrous things that my eyes have seen, that my ears have heard. I will not testify of others' deeds or experiences, but I will testify of how you have saved me from the pit and the snare of the enemy. Lord, it is embarrassing for me to have to admit before the world that I have been caught up in sexual sin. Yet, I will testify because I am compelled to speak of your mercy and deliverance.

Will you tell of God's goodness to you?
Luke 21:13-15, Acts 26:22, Acts 22:14-15, Matthew 10:32-33

AUGUST 18

Text: *Isaiah 50:7: Because the sovereign Lord helps me, I will not be disgraced. Therefore, have I set my face like flint, and I know I will not be put to shame.*

Lord, I have set my face like flint, and I write of my shame; I stand and wait, trusting in your mercy and goodness to keep me and those that I love from being vilified. I will not cower; I will not turn away from the threats of Satan and the world. But rather, I will weather their taunts and scorn trusting that you will give me your mercy and grace. I truly believe, Lord, that you would have me share about my sin with the world, so that some in the world would be helped in slipping loose from their bondage. Lord, I know that you will keep us safe.

Will God protect you from the world's taunts?
2 Thessalonians 3:3, Psalm 59:1, Psalm 91:15, Hebrews 13:6

AUGUST 19

Text: *John 15:27: And you also must testify, for you have been with me from the beginning.*

Jesus is talking to his disciples, and He tells them that they "must" testify. It will be scary, and they may even face persecution and death for testifying about Him, but they "must" testify. I have not walked with Jesus in human form as the disciples did, and for the first thirty-five years of my life I had no real relationship with Jesus. But there was a beginning to our relationship, and I must testify now to the journey on which He has led me. Will it result in persecution? Probably. Do I have a choice about whether or not I will testify? No. I "must" testify.

Must you testify?
Acts 20:22-24, 1 Corinthians 9:16, Luke 19:37-40, 1 John 4:13-14

AUGUST 20

Text: *John 18:20: "I have spoken openly to the world," said Jesus.*

God spoke openly; He spoke the truth. He was not hesitant to speak; He was not afraid of offending someone. He simply spoke the truth openly. I have not the courage that my Lord had. I am afraid. I am fearful of offending the world and, if I do, the world will not like me. I am afraid that the world will persecute me as they persecuted Jesus. I am afraid that my family and loved ones may suffer because of what I do and say. And yet, I must speak openly to the world. Jesus did and then said to me in his word, "Go and do likewise."

Will you speak truth?
Proverbs 12:22, Ephesians 4:25, 1 Peter 3:10, Psalm 34:12-14

AUGUST 21

Text: *Acts 23:11: Take courage! As you have testified about me in Jerusalem, so you must also testify in Rome.*

In the world's economy, when we have done well through great effort, we are often rewarded by some time off to rest, and we are congratulated on doing a good job. In God's economy, because Paul had done well, having been threatened, intimidated, and jailed, but having continued to faithfully testify, he is rewarded with a promise of further hardship and suffering in Rome. The encouragement and blessing was that God spoke to him, God was present with him, and he was reassured that he was serving God. His reward was that he was able to speak God's truth. Lord, let me find joy in testifying of what you have done for me.

Can you find joy in trials?
James 1:2-4, Psalm 94:19, 1 Peter 4:14, Acts 7:34-36

AUGUST 22

Text: *1 Kings 22:16: How many times must I make you swear to tell me nothing but the truth in the name of the Lord?*

Micaiah, knowing what all of the other prophets (about 400 of them) were saying, and also knowing what the king obviously wanted to hear, lied to the king and promised God's victory. The king didn't buy it; he knew that Micaiah was lying to him. Perhaps it was because Micaiah never brought him good news; perhaps it was the way in which Micaiah spoke; perhaps Micaiah was a lousy liar. In any event, the king commanded him to testify truthfully. He did and, because he did, he was thrown into solitary confinement. How many times do I ignore God's truth because I tell people what they want to hear? How many times do I pull my punches, or say nothing at all, because I am afraid of the consequences of speaking truth? Lord, I am not a prophet but I, too, must speak your truth.

Do you compromise God's truth?
James 4:17, Romans 1:25, Deuteronomy 4:2, Proverbs 25:26

AUGUST 23

Text: *John 10:25: Jesus answered, 'I did tell you, but you do not believe.*

The religious leaders of Jesus's time asked Jesus to make a flat statement to them. Either you say you are the Messiah or tell us you are not the Messiah. So, Jesus responds by telling them that He had already responded to their question and their challenge. Jesus had not only told them as He taught them but had demonstrated his divinity in what He had done. The very people who asked the question of Him had seen the miracles that He had performed. The problem wasn't that Jesus hadn't responded to their question: it was that they didn't like the answer. They didn't believe what He had told them, and they doubted what their own eyes had seen. They would never know the truth because they had chosen to believe the lie. There are a lot of lies for me to believe in today, Lord, but help me to know the truth.

> *Do you want to believe God?*
> *John 20:27-29, Ephesians 1:18-19, 1 Peter 1:8, Psalm 46:10*

AUGUST 24

Text: *John 18:38: "What is truth?" Pilate asked.*

Pilate asks the question that so many ask today. It seems that even in Jesus' day there was relativism. There was for Pilate no right, there was no wrong, just shades of good and evil, and man determines what is best for him, depending on the circumstances at the time. Pilate asked, "What is truth?" with Truth standing before him. Pilate judges truth and sees only a shade of gray. There is truth, absolute truth, and it is Jesus. I condemn Pilate and yet I, too, judge the truth on occasion from the gray standards of my world. Jesus stands before me, the Truth, and I judge the truth by a standard of relativity. He speaks to me of my sin, and I make excuses. Forgive me, Lord.

> *Do you make excuses for sin?*
> *John 15:22, Romans 2:1, Genesis 3:13, Proverbs 26:17*

AUGUST 25

Text: *1 John 5:10: …the one who does not believe God has made him a liar… (NASB)*

Satan is the liar; God cannot lie, not even a small white lie to avoid hurting someone's feelings. And what is the truth that God speaks? He says that if I repent of sin, He forgives me. He says that He has come that I may put my sin aside and live righteously. He says that I am to follow after Him and reject the temptations of the world. If, after I have prayed to receive Him, I fall back into sin, and if I believe that God cannot overcome the sin and temptation of the world, and if I believe his death on the Cross is insufficient to cover my sin and that He has not made for me a way of escape from temptation, then I make God a liar. I must not ever believe the lies of Satan but rather trust the truth of God.

> *Do you believe Satan's lies?*
> *2 Corinthians 11:3, John 8:43-44, Genesis 3:1-5, 2 Corinthians 10:5*

AUGUST 26

Text: *Proverbs 12:22: The Lord detests lying lips, but he delights in men who are truthful.*

There are many ways to lie but only one way to be truthful. The most obvious way to lie is to deliberately tell another person something that is not true. Even if my motivation is good in telling the lie, it is better to remain silent. But the more common way to lie is called hypocrisy. It is living my life so that the world sees me as one kind of person, while in secret I am not that person at all. I go to church on Sunday and pretend that my life is righteous, while I sin in secret and hope that no one will find out. If I do this long enough, I become secure in the lie, and then I begin to justify the lie and even lie to myself, and eventually I believe the lie. When the lie is full-grown, it takes over and I am a slave to Satan, the ultimate liar. But God detests any lie and knows the truth about me. I must abandon the lie and be truthful with the world, with myself, and especially with God.

Are you lying to God?
Proverbs 17:7, Jeremiah 17:9-10, Psalm 5:4-6, 1 Timothy 4:1-2

AUGUST 27

Text: *Psalm 82:2: How long will you defend the unjust and show partiality to the wicked?*

How then shall I know who is just or who is wicked? This current age is very much a time when right and wrong have become relative terms, and therefore the righteous and the wicked become relative also. Have I not said, "I am not as bad as he is," or "Yes, I sin, but so does everyone else," or "My sin is accepted and acceptable in my culture?" How then shall I tell what is unjust and what is wicked? God's law is not relative. It has not, and will not, change. God has told me in his holy word what is wicked and what is unjust, and I am to judge myself by the standard of his word, not by what anyone else, or the world, may tell me. God's word is clear.

Does the world influence what you believe?
Colossians 2:8, Romans 12:2, 1 Corinthians 3:18-20, 1 John 4:1-3

AUGUST 28

Text: *Luke 8:47: In the presence of all the people, she told why she had touched him and how she had been instantly healed.*

As difficult as it was to do so, she told the crowd why and how. Why was she required to do this? She had suffered a horrible disease and had been branded as "unclean" by those who knew her--even by her own family. It was embarrassing for her to stand in front of all these people and share with them her twelve years of shame and degradation. Besides, Jesus knew everything, even as he asked; why did he call upon her to testify? Perhaps she needed to testify so that her healing might be complete. There is a certainty, a completeness, that only comes about when we confess something aloud to the world. It sets the healing in stone, that we might not return that way again, and so that God is glorified. God has touched me and healed me. I must go to His people and confess my healing, for my sake, and for God's glory.

> *Will you admit your sin?*
> *Proverbs 28:13, James 5:16, Acts 19:18, Mark 1:4-5*

AUGUST 29

Text: *Luke 12:2: There is nothing concealed that will not be disclosed, or hidden that will not be made known.*

How foolish my addiction made me. The lie of the enemy, of my flesh, of the world, is that I can be anonymous. I follow my own temptations to places where no one knows me and believe the lie that I have gotten away with something. I commit sinful acts alone, and have lustful thoughts in a locked room, or sitting in front of a computer screen, and I am deluded into thinking that no one knows and no one will ever know. I wrap myself in the poor comfort of secrecy and anonymity and fool myself into believing that no one will ever find out. But God's word is very clear. He does not lie to me, and it is not difficult to understand. If I choose the way of sin, there is nowhere to run or to hide from the truth.

Do you hide from the truth?

Jeremiah 23:23-24, Genesis 3:8-9, Isaiah 29:15, Psalm 90:18

AUGUST 30

Text: *Revelation 11:4&5: These are the two olive trees and the two lampstands that stand before the Lord of the earth. If anyone tries to harm them, fire comes from their mouths and devours their enemies.*

This word, I believe, speaks of prophets of God's word. The olive trees speak the truth of the peace of God and Jesus' love. Lampstands, unable to be extinguished, speak truth no matter who objects or discounts the truth of God. It would seem that the world is opposed to them, because the world and the enemy do not want to hear God's truth. But the prophets are given power in their speech to totally destroy the concepts and ideas and words of the world by speaking truth. Just as Jesus answered Satan in the temptation in the desert, so will these great prophets answer Satan in the last days, speaking not from their own wisdom, strength, and power but rather speaking God's truth. I must have the courage to speak truth today as these prophets will speak it in the end times.

Do you speak truth to the world?

Zechariah 8:16, Proverbs 12:17, 2 Timothy 2:15, Proverbs 30:5-6

AUGUST 31

Text: *Luke 10:29: But he wanted to justify himself, so he asked Jesus, "And who is my neighbor?"*

The question came from one who was an expert in the religious law. Because he was an expert, he probably knew the answer to his question, but he also knew that he could debate the meaning since he and his fellow experts had probably debated the issue many times before. He was not really seeking an answer but was trying to make himself look good in the eyes of his fellow men. But Jesus surprised him and showed him the true meaning of the law, which was something that the religious leaders would not admit. Do I do this with Jesus? There are many things from God that are hidden in my heart. I know they are right and good, but they go against the traditional teachings of my world. Do I ask God about what I should do when I already know what is right but don't really want to obey? I cannot justify temptation by asking a question to which I already know the answer.

Do you try to justify disobedience?
Hebrews 10:26, James 4:17, Galatians 6:7, Galatians 5:4

SEPTEMBER

SEPTEMBER 1

Text: *Ecclesiastes 3:3: ...a time to kill and a time to heal...*

There is a time for me, and for all of us, to kill our flesh and its desires, to kill the temptations of the world. Oh, that it would be a quick death, a swing of the broadsword blade and the old man beheaded. But for me it is a slow and lingering death, not a quick experience. There is, perhaps, a reason for this. If the death were quick, I might not remain dead to my sin. But, rather, there is a season of death and a season of healing. It takes much time in my life, but God helps me and insures that the death is complete and that the healing is also complete. It is not quick, nor is it easy, but it is to be done God's way, which is always the right way.

Is your sin nature dying?
Galatians 5:24, Luke 9:23-24, Galatians 2:20, 1 Peter 2:24-25

SEPTEMBER 2

Text: *Joshua 10:19: But don't stop! Pursue your enemies, attack them from the rear and don't let them reach their cities for the Lord, your God, has given them into your hand.*

God had just performed a battlefield miracle. He kept the sun shining, and time stopped for twenty-four hours. He did this, at Joshua's request, so that the enemy might be totally destroyed, as God had ordained, and so that none of the enemy could sneak away under cover of darkness. But now the soldiers were getting tired and were being tempted to allow the enemy to just flee so that God's army could rest. But God said no; take them now while I have delivered them into your hand. God has delivered the demons that have plagued me in sin into my hand, and He tells me to utterly destroy them. I must chase them down and attack them even though I become weary. I must destroy my enemy, Satan, and his demons that have attacked me even now as God has delivered them into my hand, lest they live to war against me again.

Do you grow weary in the fight?

Psalm 73:26, 2 Corinthians 12:9, Philippians 4:13, Isaiah 40:29-31

SEPTEMBER 3

Text: *1 Kings 2:6: So act according to your wisdom, but don't let his gray hair go down to the grave in peace. (NASB)*

King David is dying. He commands his son, Solomon, who will succeed him as king, to kill Joab, who was David's enemy and who had proven treacherous. At first glance I wondered why David harbored such malice and hatred in his heart as he lay on his deathbed. But I believe that God is showing me in this passage that David is not acting out of anger or bitterness. He was making God's kingdom safe for Solomon, because he knew the evil that this man was, and the harm that he was capable of bringing. As my "old man" dies, may my new king kill the old habits and temptations that arise from my old kingdom.

Did the old man's death leave a remnant of sin?

Colossians 3:2-3, Romans 6:11-12, 1 John 1:9, 2 Corinthians 7:1

SEPTEMBER 4

Text: *Romans 8:13: For if you live according to the sinful nature, you will die; but if by the Spirit you put to death the misdeeds of the body, you will live.*

As we all do, I have a physical body that will someday perish and my soul will enter into the spiritual realm as my life here on Earth ends.

163

The spirit now dwells in my flesh and blood but, when I die, I will no longer have to contend with the evil that is also resident in my flesh. But until I die, the flesh wants its own way and fights against the Spirit for control of my actions and thoughts. But God has promised me that His spirit can be, and will be, triumphant, even while my flesh lives. It is my choice. I must die to sin, or I will die in sin.

Are you in the fight?

2 Peter 2:9-10, Romans 6:6-7, Colossians 3:7-8, James 4:17

SEPTEMBER 5

Text: *Colossians 3:5: Therefore, consider the members of your body as dead to immorality, impurity, passion, evil desire and greed, which amounts to idolatry.*

I am to think of the members of my body as dead to sin. It is so hard for me because my flesh is still alive. But even so, my mind must be stronger than my body, my heart stronger than my worldly passions. I would never go to a satanic church or a place where people worship Ashtoreth or any other idols. Clearly, that would be a betrayal of my relationship to God and a repudiation of everything I believe and for which I stand. But God's word tells me that when I allow my members to be resurrected in fleshly temptation, I worship idols. I must kill the old man.

Are there idols in your life?

1 Corinthians 10:7, Revelation 9:20-21, Psalm 16:4, 1 John 5:19-21

SEPTEMBER 6

Text: *Psalm 119:133: Direct my footsteps according to your word; let no sin rule over me. (NASB)*

My sin was my ruler and my master. It didn't start out that way. It was a diversion, a place to go when I was bored, lonely, or upset. But it grew as I fed it, and I found that I was feeding it more often. As the sin grew, I lost my fear of it. It became familiar and known and a part of me. It was, after all, MY sin. I had allowed its birth in my life and had nurtured it until it was no longer unattractive--until I thought it was my friend. But it kept growing and became a monster that directed my every thought. I could not resist the will of the beast I had created. But God has slain the beast and led me out of the dark forest where we dwelled. Lord, guide each footstep on my path to freedom with you.

Who is your master?
1 Peter 2:16, John 12:25-26, Luke 6:46, Psalm 123:2

SEPTEMBER 7

Text: *Luke 12:15: Watch out! Be on your guard against all kinds of greed; a man's life does not consist in the abundance of his possessions.*

It doesn't? I thought it did. Just like my sexual addiction, this was another lie that the enemy built into my life. It is the way I was raised; it was what I learned and what I must now abandon. I always thought, really believed, that financial success was hugely important. In fact, I grew up thinking that the whole object of my life, my whole goal, was to be successful, to have nice things, big houses, exotic cars, and great vacations. I grew up thinking that God was just a part of my life that created a Sunday obligation. But Lord,

165

now I have given my life to you, and I know intellectually that you are more important than the world, but my old habits of living in the flesh and the desire for money and things have not completely died. The things of the world are not bad, unless I let them take your place in my life. I need to put that to death in me. I need to kill it.

Is wealth your god?

1 Timothy 6:10, Matthew 6:19-21, Hebrews 13:5, Psalm 37:16-17

SEPTEMBER 8

Text: *Jeremiah 18:6: Like clay in the hand of the potter, so are you in my hand.*

I am indeed like clay in God's hand. I have impurities and faults in me just as clay does. But who am I to resist the potter's hand? Whether God breaks me into chards to reform me, or whether God is pleased with me at any given time, it is up to God. I cannot control God's pleasure or displeasure with me. I can only try to be obedient and submit to his hand. I am simply God's clay and, if I allow him to, He will mold me to His will.

Do you resist God's will?

Ephesians 2:10, Romans 9:20-21, Galatians 5:16-17, Jonah 1:1-3

SEPTEMBER 9

Text: *Jeremiah 27:5: With my great power and outstretched arm I made the earth, and its people, and the animals that are on it, and I give it to anyone I please.*

The Earth and all that are within it belong to God. God, and God alone, is in control. He is the Creator. Do I presume to think that I am in control of anything that has been created by God? Yet, God has placed things, including my sexuality, in my possession for safekeeping, and I must be a conscientious and grateful steward of what he has entrusted to me. Let my actions justify your trust in me Lord.

What do you do with God's gift?

James 1:17, 1 Peter 4:10, Romans 11:29, Matthew 25:14-18

SEPTEMBER 10

Text: *Genesis 40:8: Do not interpretations belong to God?*

The Lord is the only one who knows fully what takes place in my life. Only God can interpret what is good and what is bad in my life. I often try to figure out my life. I ask God what is good, and what does this mean and what does that portend for me and for my family. But only God knows, and so I commit my life into the hands of God, for He will do what is best for me and for those that I love. I will endeavor to obey God's word and His voice, and the rest is in God's hands.

Who is in control of your life?

Romans 8:9, Jeremiah 29:11, Psalm 9:10, Proverb 19:21

SEPTEMBER 11

Text: *Genesis 47:19: Give us seed so that we may live and not die, and that the land may not become desolate.*

God's people faced a tough choice. There was famine in the land, and they could choose to go to Pharaoh to get provision and become enslaved to Pharaoh, or they could refuse to go to Pharaoh and starve to death--and Pharaoh would get their land anyway. I feel so often that my life and the lives of my people are in a time of spiritual famine, and only God has the riches of the Holy Spirit that will keep us alive in this time of need. I gladly surrender to the Lord, and I gladly go into bondage as long as God is my master, and in exchange God gives me spiritual enrichment. If I do not surrender to God, my soul will surely die from spiritual starvation, and I will lose my peace and joy and the presence of the Holy Spirit as well. Surrendering everything I have in exchange for everything that God will give me is not such a hard decision after all.

Are you spiritually hungry?

Matthew 5:6, Psalm 63:1, John 6:35, Psalm 107:9

SEPTEMBER 12

Text: *Exodus 15:13: In your unfailing love you will lead the people you have redeemed.*

God leads me and guides me because of His great love for me. Sometimes--no, often--I am like a wayward, stubborn goat that goes everywhere but where the shepherd wants it to go; but God never stops shepherding. He never abandons me to my own pursuits, and He does not put me into a pen. But instead He allows me freedom and, as a result, I have the capability to wander off. I think that it's a lot more work for God, but it teaches me about the dangers of the world so that someday, perhaps, I might safely lead others, even as a lead goat. Thank you, Lord, for always leading, never pushing. Thank you for never giving me over to the world but always finding me when I stray. Lord, make me a better follower.

Do you stray from God?

Psalm 119:176, Proverbs 21:16, Isaiah 53:6, 1 Peter 2:25

SEPTEMBER 13

Text: *Judges 4:9: But because of the way you are going about this, the honor will not be yours...*

B arak had been given God's word and God's direction, but he decided to do things his way instead of the way that God had directed. The job still got done because God decreed that it would be so, but in doing things his own way instead of God's, Barak forfeited the blessing that God would have bestowed on him. How often do I do the same thing? I know what God wants me to do and I know how He wants me to do it. But I am afraid; I don't trust God enough to do it His way. I succumb to my fear and insecurity and do it the way I think will work best. Lord, forgive me for even thinking that I know better than you. Could I ever elevate myself to greater knowledge or higher wisdom than you? Of course not. Lord, help me to obey--your way.

Will you do it God's way?
Isaiah 55:8-9, Romans 11:34-36, Proverbs 3:5-6, John 8:12

SEPTEMBER 14

Text: *1 Chronicles 10:13: Saul died because he was unfaithful to the Lord.*

S aul committed suicide, but he did not take his own life; it was taken from him by God. Saul was disobedient to God; he attempted to do things his own way. He tried to secure his future as king. Saul did not trust God, nor did he trust in God. He tried to kill David, the future king chosen by God. God knew that Saul would not willingly give up his own desires, plans, and pride, and so Saul's life was ended. Lord, I surrender my life to you and pray that I will not get in the way of what you want to do. Once I determine that I will not do God's will, His purpose for my life is finished.

Do you interfere with God's will?
Isaiah 1:3, Proverbs 24:21-22, Acts 7:51-53, Galatians 5:7-8

SEPTEMBER 15

Text: *Job 37:7: He seals the hand of every man, that all men may know his work. (NASB)*

The writer speaks in the context of a storm and points out that God still, to this day, sends or allows to be sent, storms, hurricanes, tornados, rain, wind, snow and ice, and man's hands are "sealed." There is nothing that any man can do to prevent the storm or stop it. It will follow its own path of devastation and destruction and man cannot control it. We simply must take cover and ride it through. It does no good to be angry at the storm, to shake your fist at it, to question it or to determine not to give in to it. The storm doesn't care. So am I in my spiritual storms, Lord. I ride them out but only in the hiding place that is you.

Who is your refuge in the storm?
John 16:33, Psalm 50:15, Nahum 1:7, 1 Peter 5:6-7

SEPTEMBER 16

Text: *2 Corinthians 5:14: For the love of Christ controls us. (NASB)*

This truth of Christ, given to us in his holy word, can perhaps be read in two different ways. Both ways of reading or understanding this passage I believe to be true--or at least for me they should be. First, I know that if I belong to Christ, I am controlled by His love for me. He loves me enough to die for me, that I may be reconciled to Him, to bless my life, and to protect me in my struggle in this world. He does all this because He loves me. But I believe that the passage might also be read to mean that I am controlled, my actions are governed, my life is ordered because of His great love for me. In all that I do each day, I must be motivated because of a desire to bless God, to honor Him, and to be obedient to Him in gratitude for His love for me.

Why do you bless God?
Psalm 103:1-2, Luke 1:68, Psalm 134:1-3, 1 Peter 1:3-5

SEPTEMBER 17

Text: *Psalm 44:8: In God we make our boast all day long, and we will praise your name forever.*

I have known the presence of the enemy. He surrounded my camp and I was helpless. I could feel his glee as he anticipated his victory and the plundering of my soul. All was lost; I was ready to raise the white flag of surrender. But then I saw the mighty hand of the Lord as it reached down and swept the enemy away as if they were no more than annoying insects. I can take no credit for my rescue or for my salvation. I will not stand among my brothers and boast that my own strength outwitted the enemy. I cannot. But I will boast of God's might and power and mercy. I will boast of God's total control over me and my life. I will boast forever with each breath I take of what God has done for me.

Of what do you boast?
Ephesians 2:8-9, Psalm 44:6-8, 1 Corinthians 1:31, Galatians 6:14

SEPTEMBER 18

Text: *Genesis 2:18: Then the Lord God said, "It is not good for the man to be alone; I will make a helper suitable for him."*

I lived separated from the wisdom of God's words for the majority of my life. I have been married for many years to the wife of my youth, the most wonderful woman in the world. And yet, I have chosen to be alone. It wasn't anything that my wife had done: it was me. I believed the lie of the enemy and hid in my isolation because of my fear that I would not be loved. I am just now learning how to live in God's word, which tells me it is not good to be alone. I pray that as my relationship to my wife improves, I will truly reach the point at which I will no longer live alone. Thank you, Lord, for the gift that my wife is to me. She is flesh of my flesh, bone of my bone, my best friend, my companion, the one I love.

Are you alone?
Matthew 19:6, Luke 11:17, Ecclesiastes 4:9-13, Matthew 28:20

SEPTEMBER 19

Text: *Deuteronomy 11:26: See, I am setting before you today a blessing and a curse.*

Even as I read this passage, I am mindful of a time of temptation that is surely and inevitably coming upon me. God's holy word shows me that I have a choice. God has delivered me from an abiding sin in my life, but very soon the enemy will place before me the opportunity to return to that sin. Will I deliberately separate myself from God and isolate myself from Him? I know the temptation is coming upon me. Can I fight my way past the temptation and continue in my walk with the Lord? In the past the enemy did not have to offer much to buy me, to seduce me; I was like a cheap whore.

Lord, let me choose to stay with you, not leave you. Let me staunchly refuse to sell my soul to temptation, but let me not try to do it alone in my isolation. Help me, Lord, to surrender this to you.

Will you choose blessing or curse?
Hebrews 12:16-17, James 4:17, Genesis 4:7, Psalm 19:13

SEPTEMBER 20

Text: *Deuteronomy 28:54: Even the most gentle and sensitive man among you will have no compassion on his own brother or the wife he loves or his surviving children...*

My disobedience is an affront to God, leading to selfishness, resulting in further disobedience. As I fall into disobedience, I become selfish; I think about me instead of about God and his people. I become my own god. My selfish wants and desires become the god I worship day and night, and I don't think about or care about the wife that God has given to me and whom I love. I don't think about others, and I don't think about God, but rather I am consumed by what I want. I am tempted continually by the pleasures of the flesh that will never be satisfied. Lord, don't allow me to tread the path of disobedience and selfishness, for that way leads only to death. Lead me, Lord, to the path of caring and obedience.

Are you selfish?
James 3:16, Romans 2:7-8, Philippians 2:3-4, Matthew 6:19-21

SEPTEMBER 21

Text: *2 Kings 15:5: The Lord afflicted the king with leprosy until the day he died, and he lived in a separate house.*

God's word says that he afflicted him with leprosy. Today we are tempted to say that God allowed him to be afflicted. The word of God is not to be altered and if God afflicted him there must have been a reason for that. He was still king, but he lived alone without the touch of others, and even when he died he was not buried with his fathers but near them. He was an outcast, unacceptable, and unaccepted. I don't know what that would be like, but I know a little. My isolation was not an affliction from God--it was self-inflicted. I chose to isolate because of the fear that others would hurt me, and so I was alone. God, however, reached out to me and drew me out of my isolation and my fear. The Father's touch was truly all I needed, and I am so grateful that I will not die unacceptable and unaccepted.

Do you separate yourself from God?
Romans 8:35, Isaiah 59:2, Ephesians 4:17-18, Colossians 1:21-22

SEPTEMBER 22

Text: *Job 27:8: For what hope has the godless when he is cut off, when God takes away his life?*

When I cut myself off from God I am without hope. I have just come through a short season of sin and hopelessness, and it is so good to be home again. When I am tempted and when I fall into sin--when I turn to the world--I climb within myself and pull the ladder up behind me so that no one else can get near me. I am alone and my sin has cut me off from God and from my loved ones. My life is taken away. I have locked out God and the Holy Spirit and lost the life that they bring to me. But now I am home. Hold me and heal me, Father.

Do you hide from God?
Genesis 3:8-9, Psalm 139:7-10, Psalm 69:5, Jeremiah 23:24

SEPTEMBER 23

Text: *Proverbs 18:1: An unfriendly man pursues selfish ends; he defies all sound judgment.*

Today it's called isolating. I get hurt. I feel abandoned. I don't get my own way and I draw inside myself and shut down my emotions and become an "unfriendly" man. I trust no one and I share nothing with anyone. I separate myself, and then because of the lack of human touch, the lack of love or intimacy, I fill the void with sin. I may fill it with drinking, sexual sin, or even with overeating. And then I find that I enjoy the moment of sin and again flounder in it. Sound judgment, God's wisdom, says to stop, to feel the emotions, to reconnect to those I love. I must stop substituting sin for what I really desire and need. I must stop, listen to God's word, and reconnect.

Are you at peace?

Psalm 4:8, Psalm 119:165, John 14:27, 1 Thessalonians 5:13-15

SEPTEMBER 24

Text: *Psalm 22:11: Do not be far from me for trouble is near and there is no one to help.*

Trouble is near. It seems that trouble is never far off. There is constant temptation from the enemy and the world. Everywhere I look there are things that feed my fleshly eyes. There are many who are eager to help me. They all mean well and they desire what is best for me, but they all have their own battles to fight, and I cannot intrude upon their world. Instead, I retreat into my own dark corner and determine that I will wage war against the enemy in my own strength. I cannot do this anymore. I have no strength left. If I do not flee to God I will fall to the enemy. I know, Lord, that you are never far from me. Help me to be not far from you.

On whose strength do you rely?

Psalm 29:11, Philippians 4:12-13, Psalm 37:39-40, Isaiah 33:2

SEPTEMBER 25

Text: *Luke 6:38: For with the measure you use, it will be measured to you.*

Since I am in the process of recovery from sin and addiction, why am I so tough on others trapped in sin? I sometimes see sin in others and, like the publican, I say, "Lord, thank you I'm not like that man." Sometimes I think to myself, "See, he is not even trying to stop his sin, and it costs me so great a price to battle my own sin." On occasion I will shun the sinner for fear that I will be tempted to return to my sin, or because my reputation might be tarnished. God says to me that He has forgiven me much, and I more than anyone else must forgive. But it is not enough to forgive; I must see those trapped in sin even as God sees them. God sees the sin and despair in them as He has seen in it in me. I must see in others what I have faced. God weeps for them, and I must weep with God.

Are you compassionate?

Colossians 3:12-13, Psalm 145:9, 2 Corinthians 1:3-4, Ephesians 4:32

SEPTEMBER 26

Text: *Luke 5:32: I have not come to call the righteous, but sinners to repentance.*

This is the way in which God can use me. I know that I am not righteous, and will never be righteous, except for the righteousness imputed to me by Jesus in His mercy and grace. I must never think of myself as a godly man in my own efforts, or as a man that God has called to go to those in sin. I must know that I am the sinner that He has called to be available, in His

176

power, to reach out to those who surround me in this world. I am not better than they are; I am not to be their teacher; I am not to be their leader. I am one of them, but one to whom you have given your grace and mercy, so that in the midst of my battle I might reach out to encourage others.

Do you think you're better than others?

Philippians 2:3, Romans 12:16, Proverbs 30:12, 2 Corinthians 10:12

SEPTEMBER 27

Test: *2 Samuel 1:25: How the mighty have fallen in battle! Jonathan lies slain on your heights.*

King Saul, Jonathan's father, was out of the will of God, and God's hand of protection was withdrawn from him. He met a fitting end, dying in battle, even taking his own life. Jonathan was faithful to David, who had God's blessing, and he appeared to be faithful to God also. But Jonathan chose to cast his lot with Saul, who had lost God's protection for himself and his family. Who am I allied with who has not God's protection? Who do I trust to lead me who will lead me to spiritual death? Lord, save me from trusting those who do not trust you.

In whom do you trust?

Psalm 118:8, Isaiah 2:22, Psalm 1:1-2, Proverbs 25:26

SEPTEMBER 28

1 Thessalonians 2:6: We were not looking for praise from men, not from you or anyone else.

So many of us are people pleasers. From my earliest memories I have always desired to please others so that they would like me and be my friend. Having people like me gave value to my life; it boosted my self-esteem and made me feel good about myself. There is nothing inherently wrong with being loved by others and having a great self-image, though in many cases the people I think are my friends are really not my friends at all. The problem arises when I must betray God in order to be friends with the world. Do I fail to speak the name of Jesus for fear that I will offend someone? Do I engage in worldly activities, including sin, so that I will fit in and the world will be my friend? I must be God's friend first.

Will you please man or God?

Galatians 1:10, Acts 5:27-29, John 12:42-43, John 15:18-19

SEPTEMBER 29

Text: *Proverbs 11:27: He who seeks good finds good will but evil comes to him who searches for it.*

The plain meaning of God's word is that if I seek to do good, I will be loved by others; if I seek out evil, I will certainly find it. However, another way of looking at these words is that if I seek to do good because I am trying to get others to love me, I will find neither goodwill nor good friends, because in truth I am seeking the approval of others to make me feel good rather than seeking to do God's will. If I seek after the goodwill of men rather than seeking the will of God, I will not find goodwill in my days, but rather I will find evil. God did not create me to curry favor with other people. He created me to love Him, to serve Him, and to have fellowship with Him. I cannot strive for fellowship with God and the world at the same time. I must choose whom I will serve.

Do you seek God or the world?

Matthew 6:24, Matthew 6:33, James 4:4, 1 John 2:15-17

SEPTEMBER 30

Test: *Proverbs 12:26: A righteous man is cautious in friendship, but the way of the wicked leads them astray.*

"Cautious in friendship." We must distinguish between being friendly and having friendship. We should all be friendly. We should all extend our hand to all we meet and offer to help the downtrodden. We should smile in greeting rather than turning our backs to strangers with a frown on our faces. But we should not enter into friendship in which we pour out our hearts and reveal our souls easily or precipitously. Rather, we must search out God in the other before entering into friendship. The wicked, however, lie down with whomever they wish without much thought. Their minds do not comprehend the very nature of friendship because they are not thinking of the other person but only of themselves. They cannot give of themselves because they are too busy taking for themselves. Am I friendly with God or do I have a friendship with God?

Are you friends with God?

John 15:14-15, Proverbs 18:24, James 2:23, James 4:8

OCTOBER

OCTOBER 1

Text: *Proverbs 13:20: He who walks with the wise grows wise, but a companion of fools suffers harm.*

If I would be wise, I must be with those who are wise. I must listen to their words and observe their actions. I must show deference to their wisdom and heed their advice, and I must realize that they are wiser than I am, and that I am learning from them. I must learn humility and learn to listen instead of talk, for many have great wisdom to impart. If I do this I will become wise, and there will be those who will seek me out to partake of my wisdom. If I walk and play and indulge myself with foolish companions, I will become foolish. I will have no desire to learn but only to experience pleasure, and I will want to be their leader immediately for, in truth, I will be the greatest fool among them. I have a choice. I must choose wisdom.

Will you choose wisdom?

Proverbs 1:7, 1 Corinthians 1:31 James 1:5, Proverbs 3:13-18

OCTOBER 2

Text: *Proverbs 25:19: Like a bad tooth or a lame foot is reliance on the unfaithful in times of trouble.*

When you bite down on a bad tooth it brings pain that you don't feel as long as the tooth doesn't have any pressure on it. If you have a lame foot it may not hurt when you sit in an easy chair with it propped up on a hassock, but step down and put your weight on it and you will surely feel the pain. So, it is with an unfaithful friend. When all is going well, he brings you delight. You play together and have fun together, never thinking about whether your friend truly loves you for, after all, he is your friend. But let adversity come and often your friend will be your friend no longer; in fact, he may be very hard to find. If he is not loyal to you, he is probably not loyal to God either. He is not your friend. Just as you cannot eat with a broken tooth, or stand on a lame foot, you cannot rely on an unfaithful friend.

Who is your friend?

1 Corinthians 15:33, Proverbs 27:6, Proverbs 12:26, Psalm 55:12-14

OCTOBER 3

Text: *Psalms 40:4: Blessed is the man who makes the Lord his trust, who does not look to the proud, to those who turn aside to false gods.*

When I find myself in trouble, in a panic, to whom do I turn? Where do I turn? If I look to the proud to help me, I must know that they will only help me if it is to their advantage to do so. Being so naïve, I believe that they are my friends and that they care about me. But deep down I know that they care more about themselves than they do about me, and if they were to suffer harm from standing beside me, they would abandon me without hesitation. But God has already proven to me that He will never abandon me. He has shown me that He will pay the ultimate price--death on the cross--just because He is my faithful friend. Lord, when I am pressed on all sides, I will not count on unfaithful friends but on you alone.

Who can you count on?

Proverbs 19:6, Psalm 18:2, Isaiah 41:13, Psalm 62:5-6

OCTOBER 4

Text: *Proverbs 18:24: A man of many friends comes to ruin, but there is a friend who sticks closer than a brother.*

Unless you are able to tell a friend all the hidden things of the soul, he is an acquaintance and not worthy of being called a friend. But to the one to whom you reveal your darkest secrets and yet he loves you, and to the one who has told you his hidden thoughts and his past and yet you love him, this one is your friend. You may have many acquaintances, but you will have few friends. It is hard to share with anyone the demons that have taken up residence in your soul. But unless you tell someone about them, they will stay there forever. A friend listens to their shrieks and stands as a strong post to lean on while the demons are cast out. But he who is not a friend will not be able to stand because the demons inside of him will flee from your demons. I have a friend.

Who loves you?
John 15:13, Galatians 6:2, 1 Samuel 18:1-3, Proverbs 17:17

OCTOBER 5

Text: *Exodus 22:31: You are to be my holy people.*

God does not tell us only that we are to keep his law. He does not tell us just that we are to "do" or "not do." God tells us that we are to "be". I cannot become holy by "doing." I become holy by loving God. I must *become*, so that I will *be*, and if I become enough in love with him that I enter the state of being, I will then do what I am supposed to do because of who I am. I obey because of being; I do not "become" because of obedience. And yet, my flesh tempts me still to give a part of myself to the world. Help

183

me, Lord, to "become" more each day, to slay the flesh each day that I may "be" and therefore "do."

Do you try to become by "doing?"

Romans 5:1, Ephesians 2:8-9, 2 Timothy 1:9, Romans 12:1-2

OCTOBER 6

Text: *Leviticus 1:2: When any of you brings an offering to the Lord, bring as your offering an animal from either the herd or the flock.*

An acceptable offering at that time was an animal, not a fruit or a vegetable. I believe the principle that God taught was that they were to bring life to Him when they brought their offering. When I bring my offering to God, I am to bring my life and my love. I am not to bring that which has no thought, no feeling, no emotion. I am to present God with that which is living in me. I believe that God wants me, all of me, including my heart, my emotions, my very lifeblood. I am not to come to God as a mindless vegetable but as God's child--a living sacrifice. I must present to Him what I am, not what I have.

What do you bring to God?

Romans 12:1-2, Hebrews 13:15, Psalm 51:17, Hosea 6:6

OCTOBER 7

Text: *2 Kings 16:2: Unlike David his father, he did not do what was right in the eyes of the Lord his God.*

Each of the kings of Judah seems to be measured by the standard set by King David. Each succeeding king is measured by his acts, either good or bad, in comparison to the actions of King David. The judgment of success was not really about what they did but rather about who they were, which in turn determined how they led God's people. David's heart was pure. He was a man after God's own heart, and he was the standard by which all the others were measured. What I do matters only because it reflects what is in my heart. Lord, that I may be a man after your own heart.

Is your heart pure?

2 Timothy 2:22, Psalm 51:10-12, Ezekiel 36:26, Palm 24:3-4

OCTOBER 8

Text: *John 6:29: Jesus answered, "The work of God is this, to believe in the one he sent."*

The people asked Jesus, just as I ask today, "What can I do to please God?" Jesus answered them, as He answers me today, by telling us that we don't have to do anything, but that we must simply be true believers. If God's kingdom were here in this world, then we would be required to work to establish and maintain the kingdom. But God's kingdom is not in this world; rather, it is in the spiritual realm, and therefore there is nothing we can do to establish or maintain the kingdom of God except to become a part of it. We can do this only by loving God and entering into the intimate relationship He desires with us.

How can you please God?

Psalm 51:16-17, Galatians 1:10, 1 Thessalonians 2:4-6, Romans 8:8

OCTOBER 9

Text: *John 15:4: Remain in me and I will remain in you.*

God's presence in my life is dependent on my obedience. His word says very clearly that I cannot expect God and the Holy Spirit to remain in me, to abide in me, if I only come to God when it's convenient for me to do so. I cannot live in the world and practice sin and expect God to live in that world with me. I must remain in God's word; I must live and have my very life in only Him. Lord, this is so difficult for me. I cannot get there without your help.

Do you abide in God?

1 John 2:6, 1 John 3:24, Psalm 27:4, Psalm 91:1

OCTOBER 10

Text: *2 Chronicles 27:6: Jotham grew powerful because he walked steadfastly before the Lord his God.*

Jotham was not born into power, nor was he born powerful. He was the son of a disgraced and diseased, once-powerful king, who had fallen because of his arrogance. But Jotham grew and God helped him grow because he walked steadfastly, he took action, he did what he was supposed to do, day after day, month after month, and year after year. That is what God requires of me, that I walk steadfastly before Him, day after day, month after month, year after year. I will grow in my walk with God, but only as I abide in Him.

Are you steadfast?

1 Corinthians 15:58, Romans 5:3-4, Isaiah 26:3, 1 Corinthians 16:13

OCTOBER 11

Text: *John 15:7: If you abide in me and my words abide in you, ask whatever you wish, and it shall be done for you." (NASB)*

I want to see miracles. I want to experience healings and watch the dead rise to live again. I want to confound the enemy and say to the mountain "move" and watch as it trundles away. But I don't want to pay the price. God's word says I am to do these things, that whatever I ask He will give to me, but first I must shed everything of myself, everything that I am, and abide in Him. I cannot just come to Him to ask Him for miracles; that is not abiding. I must be with Him every day, all day. I cannot abide in the world and in God also. Only when I abide in God completely will He fulfill his promises to me.

How can we see God's miracles?
Hebrews 13:20-21, Micah 6:8, Luke 9:23, Hebrews 10:36

OCTOBER 12

Text: *Proverbs 4:34: When I was my father's son, tender and the only one in the sight of my mother, he also taught me and said to me: "Let your heart retain my word; keep my commands and live."*

God teaches me in his word and in the power of the Holy Spirit, and all wisdom comes from Him. But how do I learn wisdom from Him? I must be my Father's child. A father teaches his own child when the child is living with and learning from the father. And when he learns the commands and the knowledge that the father possesses, the child is ready to leave home and go out on his own, as long as he remembers what the father has taught. My life is to be different. God's wisdom is never-ending and never

187

exhausted, and so I can never go out on my own. Rather, I must abide in God and keep learning all the days of my life. If I were to go out on my own, I would have forgotten God's first bit of wisdom: "Abide in me."

Are you still learning?

Romans 15:4, Proverbs 1:5, 2 Peter 3:18, 1 Kings 3:5-9

OCTOBER 13

Text: *John 3:21: But whoever lives by the truth comes into the light, so that it may be seen plainly that what he has done has been done through God.*

Oh, that I would live by the truth, and the only truth is God's truth. For so many years I lived the lie that sin created when it came into my life, and the lie brought darkness to my soul. Now I must dwell in the light, and the light grows stronger each day so that I might see God's truth more clearly. The lies that I told myself and others begat more lies. Denial piled upon itself. Darkness fed darkness until the light was almost gone. I now choose to live in the light of truth and to reject the places of the deception of darkness.

Do you live in your lies?

Acts 5:4, 1 John 1:6, 1 Timothy 4:1-2, John 8:32

OCTOBER 14

Text: *Luke 11:35: See to It, then, that the light within you is not darkness."*

We all have something within us that shines out into the world. That which shines out is either the light of God or something that masquerades as light but is actually the darkness of the enemy. In this passage God describes it as "light" that I might recognize the fact that the evil I carry inside of me does radiate from within me, just as His light does, and the world sees whatever it is that I give off. I have seen it in others, this false light, and I know that others have seen it in me. Lord, take away any false light that I carry, and let there be only the pure light of you to shine from within my soul.

What does the world see in you?

Acts 7:54-56, Matthew 13:43, Daniel 12:3-4, Isaiah 3:9

OCTOBER 15

Text: *Luke 23:44: It was now about the sixth hour, and darkness came over the whole land until the ninth hour.*

God died in darkness, covered with my sin and the sin of the world. As He drew the sin of all mankind upon Him, it blotted out the sun. And the sun, even the very sun that He had created, had to stop shining at God's command, and the world appeared to have victory over God and over me. But the enemy could not triumph, even though he thought he had; the world could not remain in darkness or in sin because of God's love. Neither can I remain in darkness and sin because of God's love for me.

Do you live in darkness?

2 Samuel 22:29, Psalm 107:10, Matthew 6:23, Ephesians 5:8-10

OCTOBER 16

Text: *Exodus 14:20: Throughout the night the cloud brought darkness to the one side and light to the other side; so neither went near the other all night long.*

As the "evil empire" chased down the Israelites and was about to overtake them and return them to slavery, God intervened. He sent a pillar of cloud to separate the Israelites from their pursuers. Darkness on one side and light on the other, and neither side could cross over. Often, I feel as if this is my life. The enemy is in hot pursuit of my soul and is closing in. At these moments--no, in every moment--I need for the Holy Spirit of God to come as the cloud came and encamp between me and the enemy, between me and my sin. I must dwell in the light where the darkness cannot touch me.

Are you separated from sin?

Romans 1:1, 2 Corinthians 6:17-18, Romans 6:11-14, 1 Peter 2:9

OCTOBER 17

Text: *Exodus 27:20: To make a lamp burn continually… (NASB)*

God is the lamp that never runs out of oil. He burns continually, bright and clear in the darkness, drawing all men to His courts. Even if I saw the light and made a conscious decision to turn away, God's light would continue to burn because He is the faithful one. He is the only constant in the universe. God has drawn me and I have come to Him. And even if temptation should draw me away from the light, the light will continue to burn to guide me back into God's presence. Thank you, Lord, for your faithfulness.

Are you drawn to the light?

James 4:16, 2 Corinthians 4:6, John 3:19-21, Isaiah 9:2

OCTOBER 18

Text: *Amos 7:8: Look, I am setting a plumb line among my people Israel; I will spare them no longer.*

God has set a plumb line in his holy word, that I may know what is right and what is wrong. But I ignored the plumb line. I refused to hear God's word, and I turned my world so that it tilted toward evil. But the plumb line was still there. It mattered not if I refused to see it, or to listen; the plumb line did not depend on my eyes or ears. It was, and is, still there. God called me back into obedience, and once again I will measure my actions by the plumb line.

Which side are you on?

Joshua 24:15, Romans 8:6-8, Matthew 7:13-14, Psalm 119:30-31

OCTOBER 19

Text: *Matthew 6:23: If then the light within you is darkness, how great is that darkness.*

The light within me is the light of the Holy Spirit that dwells in the temple of my body, and in this light there is no darkness. In my temple there should be no darkness. But, if I choose to do so, I can drive the Holy Spirit from the temple. If I choose to fill myself, my body, my mind, my heart, and my soul with the idols of the world, the Holy Spirit will not stay, because the Holy Spirit of God will not dwell in the presence of evil. God has told us in His word that He would not share His temple with other gods. The word declares: "I am the Lord your God. There shall be no other gods before me." If I drive God away from me, I will dwell in utter darkness with no light to keep me from falling and harming myself. Lord, let me live in light with you.

Do you turn away from God?

Isaiah 59:2, Hebrews 10:26-27, 2 Timothy 4:3-4, 1 John 1:8-9

OCTOBER 20

Text: *1 Thessalonians 5:4-5: But you, brothers, are not in darkness so that this day should surprise you like a thief. You are all sons of the light and sons of the day.*

When I was born, I was born into darkness. My eyes were closed, and I knew nothing of God. As I grew my eyes were opened, but I still remained in darkness. I could see the light, and I was attracted to it, but I continued in darkness. The light came into my life like a lightning bolt, and suddenly I was in the light, and no longer dwelt in darkness. I have left behind the things of darkness. Sometimes, I miss those things of the world, but I will not grieve for them. Rather, I will turn my face to the light, and my back to the darkness, that I may see the Son.

Will you leave the things of the world behind?

Ephesians 4:22-24, 2 Corinthians 5:17, Colossians 1:13-14, Isaiah 43:18-19

OCTOBER 21

Text: *Psalm 5:8: Lead me, O Lord, in your righteousness because of my enemies — make straight your way before me.*

My enemies surround me like an impenetrable jungle. Sin and temptation assault me on all sides, and wherever I turn there is only the path that leads to destruction. I am lost in a world that is caught up in evil. But no matter how lost I am, and no matter how deeply the world has penetrated, I can still see God if I look for Him. God is the light that glows in the darkness, ever visible unless I turn my back to stare into the darkness. In a world of evil, God is righteous, and His righteousness goes before me and clears the path before me. If I follow the path of God's righteousness, my way through the darkness is made straight and God does lead me, day by day, with grace and mercy.

Are you on God's path?
Isaiah 59:8, Psalm 25:4-5, Hebrews 12:12-13, Psalm 16:11

OCTOBER 22

Text: *Psalm 21:4: He asked you for life and you gave it to him — length of days forever and ever.*

I have asked the Lord for life--eternal life with Him. God has blessed me with life. Why, then, do I still feel drawn to the death contained in my old temptations and habits? God has promised me life, not only in the future but for the present as well. He has shown me that I may dwell in His house and presence even now on this Earth and in this place. Knowing that God's purity and righteousness bring wholeness and abundance and light, and that my flesh craves darkness and poverty and death, why do I so often give in to the temptations of my flesh? Why do my eyes stray from God's glory to the shabbiness of the world? Lord, I ask you to give me the strength to live victoriously.

Do you live victoriously?
1 Corinthians 15:56-57, 1 John 5:3-5, 2 Corinthians 2:14, Galatians 4:6-7

OCTOBER 23

Text: *Luke 8:16: No one lights a lamp and hides it in a jar or puts it under a bed. Instead, he puts it on a stand, so that those who come in can see the light.*

I have been given much light, for I dwelt in the darkness of sexual sin. The deeper I was enmeshed, the darker it became, until the Lord God came to me and lit a match. In the total darkness even a match gives off great light. So I cupped my hand around it, protecting it, so that it would not be blown out. The light grew and became strong, and still I shielded it from the world so that the world would not suspect that I had been in the darkness. But it is not my light. It was given to me by God. I cannot keep the world from seeing the light, for God intends that the world be drawn to it. I must hold the light on high and invite the world to partake of the light and of the grace of God.

Are you hiding God's light?
Matthew 5:14-16, John 8:12, 2 Corinthians 4:6-7, John 12:35-36

OCTOBER 24

Text: *Luke 22:53: Every day I was with you in the temple courts, and you did not lay a hand on me, but this is your hour – when darkness reigns.*

Jesus, speaking to those who had come to kill God, speaks not with venom, or anger, or fear, but with great sorrow. He looks upon a crowd armed with swords and clubs who have come for the Prince of Peace. Perhaps Jesus recalls the temptation in the desert when Satan promised that there would be another time and place when he would again attack. And Jesus sees the overwhelming darkness that is beginning to enfold the whole Earth. This is the moment that Satan believes to be his triumph. For three days he will rule the

Earth, but Jesus knows that on the third day dawn will break and the darkness will be vanquished once and for all. That darkness, the darkness of Satan, has ruled over me. But Jesus weeps over me also, and delivers me from the darkness, as I look eagerly for the dawn.

Do you wait for the dawn?
Psalm 130:5-6, Matthew 28:1, Isaiah 9:2, Psalm 57:8

OCTOBER 25

Text:: *Luke 14:11: For everyone who exalts himself will be humbled, and he who humbles himself will be exalted.*

If I try to exalt myself, I will fail. First, I know who I am and I know the sin in my life, and I know that nothing that I have done deserves to be exalted. Second, if I attempt to exalt myself, I do so with a totally selfish motivation. I want glory, and I want people to like and admire me. And I am doomed to a life of ignominy. But if I humble myself, empty myself of my selfishness, I allow God to be exalted in me. As God is praised, I will be lifted up with Him. Lord, I desire no exaltation except that which is in you.

Will you give God the Glory?
Jeremiah 9:23-24, Psalm 115:1, Galatians 6:3, Galatians 6:14

OCTOBER 26

Text: *Psalm 51:2-3: Wash away all my iniquity and cleanse me from my sin, for I know my transgressions and my sin is always before me.*

I cannot ever exalt myself, for I know myself too well. I am burdened by a life in which I have continually sinned against God. God has delivered me, and I walk in His deliverance, but my past is like a huge pile of dung that

I have left behind. There it sits: it smells, it's ugly, it's filled with decay and disease. And it never goes away. Father, let it be so. No matter how far away I walk, it will be there to remind me of where I've been and of your mercy and grace.

Does God's forgiveness humble you?
Proverbs 18:12, Luke 5:31-32, 1 Corinthians 1:28-31, Psalm 25:7

OCTOBER 27

Text: *Luke 20:46: Beware of the teachers of the law. They like to walk around in flowing robes and love to be greeted in the marketplaces and have the most important seats in the synagogues and the places of honor at banquets.*

The description is of the man who likes to dress up and wants to be loved, honored, and respected by the world. I must confess that I have been that man. I must confess that I am that man. My flesh cries out for the world to love me. I feel good when I am dressed in finery. I crave the admiration and adoration of the world. There is nothing wrong with dressing well and being respected and even loved by those who know me. But, Lord, let it never be more important to me than being clothed in your Holy Spirit and having the love and respect that only you can give to me.

Who are you trying to impress?
Matthew 23:5-7, 1 Thessalonians 2:4, Luke 16:15, Philippians 2:3-4

OCTOBER 28

Text: *Exodus 10:3: How long will you refuse to humble yourself before me?*

What does it mean to humble myself before God? God has made me to be a man, a warrior. I dare not crawl to others or cower before

196

the world. But, in the presence of God, I must realize who I am and who God is, and out of the gratitude that I owe to my Lord, I must consider myself as nothing and God as everything. Moses was not particularly humble before Pharaoh, but he was exceptionally humble before God. I must be humble before God and a warrior before the world. I cannot be a warrior in the world if I am not humble before God.

How do you approach God?

Psalm 46:10, James 4:8-10, Psalm 24:3-4, Jeremiah 29:12-13

OCTOBER 29

Text: *Numbers 16:1: Korah son of Izhar, the son of Kohath, the son of Levi, and certain Reubenites—Dathan and Abiram, sons of Eliab, and On son of Peleth—became insolent and rose up against Moses.*

God's word says that they became insolent. Insolence is something more than disobedience. It is me being disobedient, knowing that I sin, and proclaiming to the world that I am not a sinner, that I am holy, and just as good as others who really do live and proclaim righteousness. Insolence is the opposite of humility. God's response to the tribes of Israel was to wipe the insolence from them by allowing them to be infected with a deadly plague. God did not tolerate insolence before him in Moses' day, and He will not tolerate it in His people today. I know that I am a disobedient sinner, and I do not pretend to be anything else. I have not yet convinced myself that I am holy; I know that I am not. But I also know that God will make me to be that which He chooses me to be.

Does arrogance lead you to insolence?

Romans 12:3, Psalm 17:10, Obadiah 1:3-4, Proverbs 21:4

OCTOBER 30

Text: *1 Samuel 18:23: I'm only a poor man and little known.*

Here was David, a shepherd, from a family that was not particularly well connected politically. He was the youngest of his family, and yet he was shown great favor by God. God often picks the least of the world to do His work. David had slain Goliath and soothed the king with his playing on the lyre. He was given wisdom and victory every time he went to battle. And yet when Saul, the king, proposed that David marry his daughter, he replied that he was not worthy. Saul, too, had been anointed by God, and had been a humble man, but he had long since forgotten both anointing and humility. Anointing and humility seem somehow to go hand in hand. Lord, I echo the words of David and say that "I am only a poor man and little known." Keep me, Lord, from anything that would cloud that reality, and use me as you will.

Do you seek fame and fortune?
1 John 2:15-17, John 12:42-43, Philippians 2:3-4, John 5:44

OCTOBER 31

Text: *1 Kings 13:33: Even after this, Jeroboam did not change his evil ways…*

Jeroboam was chosen by the hand of God to lead God's people. Sin and rebellion caught up to him. He became rich and powerful, and so it was hard for him to keep his heart pure, because the world offered him so much. As he rebelled against God, he fashioned other gods for his people, and God's people, to worship. If the people worshipped gods that Jeroboam made, then they worshipped Jeroboam, and he became their god. God showed him clearly, through prophecy and the healing of a withered hand, what was to come. But even then, he refused to lead the people back to God.

198

Lord, help me not to be a Jeroboam. Help me not to be tempted to try and take your place. Help me to worship you, and only you, in true humility.

Have you become your own god?

1 John 4:1, Romans 1:25, 1 John 5:21, Exodus 20:2-

NOVEMBER

NOVEMBER 1

Text: *2 Chronicles 6:13: He stood on the platform and then knelt down before the whole assembly of Israel and spread out his hands toward heaven.*

Here was Solomon, king of Israel, king of God's people, celebrating the completion of the building of the temple of God. He has just recounted the promise made to David, his father, and reaffirmed before all the people that God had chosen him to be their king and to build the temple where God would dwell. And then, before all of his people, and God's people, in his moment of triumph and celebration, he kneels before god. It is an example of humility; an example to Israel of how they were to live before God from the greatest of them to the least. Lord, in every triumph that you give to me, may I have the courage and strength to model humility before your people.

Do you model humility?
Matthew 4:13-16, Luke 22:25-27, John 13:3-5, Philippians 2:5-8

NOVEMBER 2

Text: *2 Chronicles 10:13: The king answered them harshly. Rejecting the advice of the elders, he followed the advice of the young men.*

What is it about youth that makes them so sure of themselves, so full of confidence in themselves, that they instinctively feel they are tougher, better, and smarter than anyone else? How does Satan play upon the arrogance of youth? Lord, I believe that is why each of us must have a breaking of our heart to know you. Without the breaking of my heart, my arrogance would still be intact. It is only when the heart is broken that the arrogance is broken also, and your word and your touch are able to penetrate the soul. My breaking was hard, but I thank God for allowing me to be broken, that I might know Him.

Have you been broken?

Psalm 51:17, Matthew 21:44, Matthew 5:3, Psalm 34:18

NOVEMBER 3

Text: *Daniel 4:34: Then I praised the Most High; I honored and glorified him who lives forever.*

Daniel praises God, not only for his deliverance from the fire but also because he had proven to king Nebuchadnezzar that Daniel's God was God of all. And the king called Daniel the one who was filled with the spirit of the gods. The king grew arrogant as he saw the blessings that God had given him, and the arrogant king decided he had done it himself. The Lord visited humility upon him. For seven long years he wandered, unkempt and mad, in the streets and fields as the lowest of the low. When he had been humbled God restored his kingdom to him. When I am walking in victory and times are good, I, too, begin to think that I have done it through my own strength. Lord, help me to learn so you don't have to teach me humility as you taught Nebuchadnezzar.

Who brings you victory?

Proverbs 21:31, 1 Corinthians 15:57, Psalm 60:11-12, 1 Samuel 17:47

NOVEMBER 4

Text: *Luke 14:11: For everyone who exalts himself will be humbled, and he who humbles himself will be exalted.*

God, as always, does so much better than I do. I exalt myself; I succumb to my pride and try to make myself seem important and powerful and good and godly. Why do I do this? I seek to make others respect me and love me. I should be seeking God's respect and love rather than man's. With God's respect and love I do not have to do anything to receive it except to accept it. Lord, help me stop my striving. Help me humble myself and seek only to accept your exaltation, for as I walk with you, I am exalted by you.

Do you exalt yourself?

Galatians 6:3, Romans 12:3, Proverbs 16:18-19, James 4:6

NOVEMBER 5

Text: *Luke 16:15: What is highly valued among men is detestable in God's sight.*

What is highly valued? What do I value highly? Wealth? But if I put great value on wealth, I will need a miserly and greedy attitude to amass it. God despises those attitudes but loves generosity. I desire good looks, charisma, and charm, but these things lead me to pride, and God loves a humble heart. I prize position in the world and seek admiration and deference from others, but God loves the servant. I seek after power, but God loves surrender. Lord, help me to surrender all of my worldly desires to you.

What do you value?

1 Peter 2:11, 1 John 2:16-17, Philippians 2:3, Hebrews 13:5

NOVEMBER 6

Text: *1 Timothy 3:6…he may become conceited and fall under the same judgment as the devil."*

Satan is the angel that fell from grace, that was banished from the heavens, that will spend eternity in agony. The reason for his fall was pride, arrogance, and conceit. Satan emulated God; he wanted to be like God and, ultimately, he wanted to be God. I want to be holy. I want to be empowered by God to do His will. These desires, though laudable, can become arrogance. When I am doing well, and when God is blessing me, I am in danger of having my pride tweaked, and I am tempted to try to be like God, using my own power and strength instead of God's. When I try to do God's work in my own power instead of His, I am really trying to be God instead of trying to be like God. This is arrogance and pride, and I am doing exactly what Satan did.

Do you try to do it yourself?
Proverbs 26:12, Psalm 10:4, Daniel 5:18-20, Psalm 49:13-14

NOVEMBER 7

Text: *Psalm 22:24: For he has not despised or disdained the suffering of the afflicted one; he has not hidden his face from him but has listened to his cry for help.*

God does not hate me in my infirmity, but rather He loves me and listens to me as I call out to Him to help me when my flesh and the world tempt me to turn my back on Him. I have turned a deaf ear to the afflicted. As I walk down the street, I tune out the voices of the needy that call to me. When I see someone on the street who has ravaged his or her own life with drugs, alcohol or perversion, I turn away so that I will not have to see. But you, Lord, you see and you care, and you never turn away or stop up your ears. I am no better than the most disheveled street person. If you love me enough to listen to me, how can I then look away from your children in need?

Does God love you even when you sin? Do you love others?
1 John 4:19-21, Ephesians 4:32, Matthew 10:8, Matthew 25:44-45

NOVEMBER 8

Text: *Luke 14:11: For everyone who exalts himself shall be humbled, and everyone who humbles himself shall be exalted. (NASB)*

One way or another, I will be humbled. I may choose to humble myself, or I may be stuck with being humbled against my will. If I humble myself, will I then be exalted in this world? Probably not. Will I be exalted in God's world? Absolutely! I could choose to exalt myself in this world, and I might even be good at it. There are many who tell me of their great power and wealth and talent. They are very successful at getting the attention of the world. But fame and glory last only for a time and then are gone. If we do not humble ourselves, today, we will be humbled in eternity. And when God has subdued the wild beast of sexual sin within me, I will be tempted to exalt myself. But I cannot. I must humble myself.

Will you humble yourself?
James 4:10, 1 Peter 5:6, Proverbs 3:34-35, Psalm 25:9

NOVEMBER 9

Text: *John 4:14: Everyone who drinks this water will be thirsty again, but whoever drinks the water I give him will never thirst. Indeed, the water I give him will become in him a spring of water welling up to eternal life.*

I don't believe that God's word means that I will never be thirsty for his touch; I believe it means that never again will I thirst after the salvation that I had not known. I wake thirsty in the morning. My need is for living water, and so I come to you Lord, alone, just you and me in the quiet of the first moments of my day, and you satisfy my longing. Lord, today, fill me with the water of you, that your love for me would well up from my innermost being to touch others.

Do you thirst for God?

John 6:35, Isaiah 55:1, Revelation 22:17, Psalm 42:1-2

NOVEMBER 10

Text: *Luke 19:40: "I tell you," he replied, "if they keep quiet, the stones will cry out."*

I cannot keep silent about my God today, any more than the people could when God walked among them. I am God's creation, made to praise Him. I am made to marvel at His holiness, to revel in His love, to stand in awe of His majesty, to be humbled by His presence. Lord, I cannot stand by silently because you created me to rejoice.

Do you speak God's praise?

Hebrews 13:15, Ephesians 5:19-20, Psalm 150:1-6, 1 Peter 4:11

NOVEMBER 11

Text: *Exodus 37:9: The cherubim faced each other, looking toward the cover.*

For the holy of holies, the Ark of the Covenant, the place that God's glory was to dwell, there were to be statues of two of God's created beings—angels--who would face God's dwelling place and worship God continually. I must understand that this is the highest calling to which I must aspire--to worship God continually. Help me, oh Lord, to worship you all the days of my life. Help me, Father, to worship you today.

Do you worship every day?

Psalm 71:8, Psalm 34:1, John 4:23-24, Romans 12:1

NOVEMBER 12

Text: *Leviticus 2:13: Season all your grain offerings with salt. Do not leave the salt of the covenant of your God out of your grain offerings.*

The grain offering was pleasing to God because it was the common ordinary food of his people at that time. It was the bread of life. Today it is the everyday things that I do in the normal course of my day. Everything I do should be an offering to God. I must not forget to add the salt of my covenant with God and God's covenant with me. It is what gives flavor and interest and excitement to my life. If I do my daily work without God, my day is flat and lifeless and boring. But, with God, each day is a great adventure.

Does God season your day?

1 Corinthians 10:31, Colossians 3:17, Galatians 5:25, Acts 17:28

NOVEMBER 13

Text: *2 Samuel 6:21: I will celebrate before the Lord.*

These are the words of David to his wife Michal, when she became upset and angry at him and ridiculed him because she was embarrassed at his very open and public display of emotional worship. David's response to her was simple and right and good. It didn't matter to David who was watching; it didn't matter what they thought. What mattered to David was that he was

207

worshipping God in the way that was pleasing to God, even if it wasn't pleasing to his wife. David had the courage to be obedient, and joyfully so, and faithful to God. Lord, that I might be a "David" in my worship of you; that I might set aside any thought of what others may think. That I will praise you as you show me and tell me how to bring you praise.

Are you free to worship?

2 Corinthians 3:17, Acts 16:24-25, Romans 14:11, Psalm 105:1-4

NOVEMBER 14

Text: *Nehemiah 11: 22-23: ...who were the singers for the service of the house of God for there was a commandment from the King concerning them and a firm regulation for the song leaders day by day. (NASB)*

God set aside certain people to perform specific tasks. The singers were given their assignment and called by God. It seems that this was an important calling. At least it was important enough to be part of God's word. Worship is important because it is designed to lead God's people into His presence. As I worship, often the Holy Spirit of God comes upon me, or perhaps I am able to be in a place where the Holy Spirit is manifested, and I am able to be in intimacy with God. I believe that it is God's desire that I make such contact with Him every day, and that I feel His presence daily. For on the day that I do not see God, the world is able to ravage me. Protect me, Lord. Keep me in your presence daily.

Do you need to worship God?

Jeremiah 20:13, Isaiah 29:13-14, Luke 19:37-40, Luke 4:5-8

NOVEMBER 15

Text: *Psalm 6:5: No one remembers you when he is dead. Who praises you from the grave?*

So long as God wishes to use me in this world, He will keep me safe from the grave. I will live just exactly as long as God determines to be right. And while I am here, I will praise God. I will stand in the assembly and lift my voice to God; I will kneel and pray in the public square. I will write of God's salvation and grace and mercy. And I will die when God determines that the moment is right and my voice, my praise in this world, will cease. I will not praise God from the grave because I will not remain in the ground. Rather, I will be lifted up with God and spend eternity with him, that I may praise my God forever.

Do you live a life of praise?
Psalm 63:3-4, Psalm 35:28, Psalm 104:33, Psalm 145:1-2

NOVEMBER 16

Text: *Psalm 32:11: Rejoice in the Lord and be glad, you righteous; sing, all you who are upright in heart.*

I will rejoice in my Lord and I will rejoice with Him. I will sing; I will lift my voice in prayer. I will dwell in God's thoughts in my moments of silence, and I will shout forth my delight. When I am upright in heart my joy cannot be contained. I must exult in and exalt my Lord. But it is not always so. When I dwell under the cloud of the darkness of my sin I cannot rejoice. My happiness is forfeited and there is no joy. In those times, I long for God and I long to be upright. It is then that I will confess and repent to my God and stand as an act of obedience. And in the strength of the will that God has provided, even then, I will be restored and I will rejoice.

Do you rejoice in the Lord?

Philippians 4:4, 1 Thessalonians 5:16, Psalm 68:3-4, 1 Peter 1:8

NOVEMBER 17

Text: *Psalm 35:10: My whole being will exclaim, "Who is like you, O Lord?"*

When I stand before God to praise Him, I hear the strings and the instruments. I open my mouth and repeat words that tell Him I love him. Often my soul is touched. Gifted people sing beautiful melodies and talented feet dance with waving flags, and I feel comfortable and safe and awed by God's power and presence. But it is not enough. There is still something down deep inside of me that wants to respond, but I am restrained. I want to come before my God even now and exclaim that *He is God, that He is God, that He is God,* and to feel it with my whole being. I want my bones to rejoice and my spirit to weep with joy and my heart to be in rapture of Him. For only then will I realize true healing.

Does God touch you?

Jeremiah 29:12-13, Luke 7:14-15, Romans 8:26-27, Galatians 4:6

NOVEMBER 18

Text: *Psalm 103:1: Praise the Lord, O my soul; all my inmost being, praise his holy name.*

Why do I do that? I understand that my soul praises God, and rightly so. God created me, He sustains me, He makes good and wonderful things to happen in my life and comforts me in times of trouble. Even if I had never existed God would still be God, the creator and sustainer, and worthy of all praise. But why do I praise His name? His name is a word that I call Him. He is my father, the daddy I go to as I crawl into His lap. He is the mighty warrior who battles on my behalf. He is the lawgiver who is feared, and rightly so, when I am disobedient. He is my Savior who has delivered me from the sin that ensnared me and delivers me from the punishment that I so richly deserve. When I speak the name of Yahweh, or Jesus, or Holy Spirit, it is with awe and praise, not because of the word that I speak but because I speak of Him.

Do you honor God's name?

Jeremiah 29:12-13, Matthew 7:7-8, Psalm 100:4-5, Proverbs 18:10

NOVEMBER 19

Text: *Psalm 113:2: Blessed be the name of the Lord from this time forth and forever. (NASB)*

Lord, forgive me for I have grumbled against you. I have been woebegone because of my foolish desires and I have been bereft because of my actions. Lord, I have not given you praise at these times. I was created to praise you in all circumstances, when I am joyful and when my countenance is downcast. But you do not distinguish based on my emotions, my fears, or my joy. Neither do you take into account my depression or elation. You simply tell me to praise you at all times. The greatest victory of the enemy would be to rob me of my praise for you. From now on unto eternity I will praise you, Lord, in all things, even, and perhaps especially, when I feel like crying instead of praising.

Do you praise God at all times?

Psalm 34:1, Hebrews 13:15, James 5:13, Psalm 150:6

NOVEMBER 20

Text: *Psalm 118:14: The Lord is my strength and my song; he has become my salvation.*

When I was young, in my teens, I had a song that was "my song." In all probability it had something to do with what people call "puppy love," a romantic feeling stirred by adolescent emotion. Whenever I heard it, I would feel those emotions. Now I am an adult and my song is the Lord. It is not a tune about the Lord, but the Lord himself, who I love with a mature love. Still, whenever I hear the name of Jesus, whenever I utter his name or his words, I am touched and humbled and reminded of His love and my salvation. The salvation was always there, like the tune and lyrics of a beautiful melody, but He has become my salvation as I first heard His song, and as I continue to listen to and experience the touch of the one who loves me in return, I am blessed.

Are you blessed by Jesus' name?

Philippians 2:9-11, Psalm 68:4, Malachi 4:2, Psalm 148:13-14

NOVEMBER 21

Text: *Psalm 148:1: Praise the Lord; praise the Lord from the heavens, praise him in the heights above.*

We praise God from this Earth that he created. Worship is the sound of a single voice raised in praise of God. A congregation comes together, and they lift their voices in songs of worship and in clapping and in words of exaltation. Churches come together, believers come together, and all those in this world worship God, and a great cacophony of praise comes forth from the Earth. The angels in the heavenly realms lift their praise to God constantly, and the saints gathered around Him on His throne fall before Him in adoration. All that God has created come before Him in worship, because He is the one true God, the only God, the eternal God, all powerful. Yet in the midst of all the praise, God hears me. He hears the single, solitary voice of this sinner raised in thanks and adoration to Him because he loves me.

Does God hear your voice?

Psalm 66:17-20, 1 John 5:14, Psalm 139:4, 1 Peter 3:12

NOVEMBER 22

Text: *Psalm 149:1: Praise the Lord. Sing to the Lord a new song, his praise in the assembly of the saints.*

Lord, I will praise you. My song of praise will be, and is, a new song, fresh every morning. No longer will my praise be bound and fettered by resident sin, but rather my praise will rise to you, clean and pure from a heart that overflows with love for you and does not need to have dark corners of sin swept clean. My heart, Lord, is pure before you because of what you have done. I have confessed my sin to you and to my brothers, and you have cleansed my heart and made me clean in your death and resurrection. You have knelt down and whispered in my ear that you love me, and you have made me glad, and I will praise you with the joy of my new song.

Is your heart pure before God?

Psalm 51:10-12, 1 John 3:2-3, James 4:8, Matthew 5:8

NOVEMBER 23

Text: *Revelation 19:5: Then a voice came from the throne, saying, "Praise our God, all you his servants, you who fear him, both small and great!"*

213

The very voice of God--but it is not a command. God does not command me to worship Him for, after all, true worship cannot be coerced.

I cannot truly worship God out of a sense of obligation, for then I am paying God back for what He has done for me. I cannot worship out of a sense of fear, for if I do I worship only because I have to. I cannot worship begrudgingly out of blind obedience. No, not obedience to a rule that says we are to worship, but rather I must be obedient to my God who invites me to worship Him. It is an invitation to relationship with God, to run into his arms, allowing Him to hold me and love me. It is an invitation to be in His presence. And so, I come to Him in relationship, and offer my praise because I love Him and He loves me.

Why do you worship God?

Isaiah 43:20-21, Psalm 95:6-7, 1 Chronicles 16:23-25, Matthew 22:37

NOVEMBER 24

Text: *Luke 6:21: Blessed are you who weep now, for you will laugh.*

I was one who would not weep. I thought that weeping was a sign of weakness, and I was determined to be strong. The truth, though, is that I was being closed, protective, and cloistered. I have found that it is good to weep, and that I am really strong enough not to care what anyone else thinks about my tears. If I cannot weep, if I cannot mourn, I cannot feel all the other emotions that God wants me to experience. I must be strong enough to allow others to see my emotions and, even more difficult, I must have the strength to feel the emotions. Thank you, Lord, for my tears. Thank you for turning them into laughter. Thank you for showing me how to experience your love.

Do you weep before God?

John 16:20, Psalm 126:5-6, John 11:33-35, Psalm 56:8

NOVEMBER 25

Text: *Luke 9:62: Jesus replied, "No one who puts his hand to the plow and looks back is fit for service in the Kingdom of God."*

What is done is done; I will not look back. I am not who I was. God has destroyed my ability to live in the world, as one of the world. Oh, I realize that I will face further temptation and that I may well fall, but I can no longer accept sin as a way of life. I am ruined for being what I was. I thank God, for only He could change me so utterly that I am no longer able to exist as an unclean man. I will not look back because I cannot look back. I look only forward, down the path that God has chosen for me as I walk with Him.

Are you done with your past?
2 Corinthians 5:17, 1 Peter 2:24-25, Romans 6:1-4, Psalm 103:12

NOVEMBER 26

Text: *Job 16:15: I have sewed sackcloth over my skin and buried my brow in the dust.*

I have made myself to live in the shame of my transgression and misery. I have wrapped myself in my guilt and fallen on my face, crying out to God for forgiveness and mercy. I have lived on my knees with my sin ever before me, convicting me moment by moment. But God came to me and lifted my head from the dirt. He replaced the sackcloth, which was of my own making, with soft garments of forgiveness and armor for battle. Now God commands me to stand as the warrior He intended me to be. Thank you, Lord, for showing me who I am.

Are you wearing your shame?
Psalm 38:4, 1 John 1:9, Romans 8:1-2, Hebrews 8:12

NOVEMBER 27

Text: *Micah 5:4: And they will live securely, for then his greatness will reach to the ends of the earth, and he will be their peace."*

I am one of God's people, and I will live securely because of Jesus. His great sacrifice firmly fixed his greatness in all of the Earth. His death brought forgiveness, His resurrection brought salvation, and I will have peace all the days of my life. Of course, evil is still rampant in the world, and it is becoming bolder and gaining strength every day. Evil still seeks to destroy me. But God is my peace; in Him is my victory and my great triumph.

Do you have peace?
1 Peter 3:10-11, 1 Peter 5:7, Philippians 4:6-7, John 16:33

NOVEMBER 28

Text: *Psalm 40:16: But may all who seek you rejoice and be glad in you; may those who love your salvation always say, "The Lord be exalted!"*

God did not die on the cross that I should spend my life weeping and mourning. He did not come that I might walk with bowed head, groveling in shame. He came that I might be forgiven, and I am to celebrate my salvation. I am to rejoice and be glad and give God glory. I am to have the joy of God's presence within me because my sin has been taken from me and replaced with God's Holy Spirit. I am not to let those who are self-righteous place me in a lesser position or convince me that I must remain in mourning for my sin. I am forgiven, and I rejoice and magnify God in his love for me.

Do you rejoice in your healing?
Psalm 51:12, Luke 15:7, Isaiah 61:10, John 15:9-11

NOVEMBER 29

Text: *Psalm 41:11: I know that you are pleased with me for my enemy does not triumph over me.*

Sometimes the enemy tricks me into believing that he has triumphed over me. But it is a lie; for my enemy, Satan, is a liar and cannot tell the truth. And just at the moment when I am so sorely tempted to believe his lie, when I want to give in to temptation and be carried away on the tide of disobedience, God comes to me in His power and might to show me that defeat is the lie of the enemy, and that He will keep me from being a slave to sin. God loves me, and He is pleased with me. I know this because He gives me victory over my enemies. It is God's victory, not mine, and He gives it to me. He shares His triumph with me.

Do you believe the enemy's lies?

John 8:44, 2 Corinthians 11:14, 2 Thessalonians 2:10-12, Colossians 1:13

NOVEMBER 30

Text: *Luke 10:18: I saw Satan fall like lightning from heaven.*

He was there: He saw it. He was in the battle, and He saw the defeat of Satan and his army. It is the message Jesus brings to me in a world filled with temptation and disease. It is a world that is owned by Satan and controlled by him--for now. But in this passage Jesus tells me that I am to come to Him, that He has already defeated Satan. Jesus tells me that He has thrown Satan down from heaven and, even though Satan is powerful--a former angelic being in the heavenlies--that he has defeated him in his rebellion. Jesus has given his followers authority over Satan. Does not a conqueror rule over those he defeats? Even though the enemy may still be strong and courageous and very dangerous, the conqueror doesn't fear him, for the host of God's army stands ready to come to the aid of God's people. I, too, am a conqueror in Jesus.

Do you let Satan win?
1 John 3:8, John 10:10, Romans 16:20, 1 Peter 5:8-11

DECEMBER

DECEMBER 1

Text: *Revelation 19:19: Then I saw the beast and the kings of the earth and their armies gathered together to make war against the rider on the horse and his army.*

I see the injustice and the evil and the temptations of the world, and I am sometimes filled with fear and sorrow and trepidation. The enemy even convinces me, somehow, that this is personal, that the world is doing this against me individually as I walk in my faith. I do not see that the battle fought here in this world is the battle that began in the heavenlies. It is a spiritual war. Surely, I will die and those around me will fall, but the real importance of all of this is not whether I live or die but whether I will be with the Lord or with the enemy. Two great forces are being drawn up for the final battle. Kings and rulers of the world prepare for battle against God and His spiritual kingdom. There will be a battle. God wins.

Are you ready for war?

Ephesians 6:11-12, Deuteronomy 20:1, 1 Timothy 6:12, Psalm 144:1

DECEMBER 2

Text: *Matthew 26:45: Look, the hour is near, and the Son of Man is betrayed into the hands of sinners.*

I am guilty of taking the life of my Lord Jesus. Each and every sin that I have committed drove a spike through His body and into the cross. I killed Him. If I think about Jesus' death in the abstract, it becomes imper-sonal. It becomes a theoretical concept and not a reality. But Jesus died will-ingly to forgive my sins and to bring to me His grace, mercy and love. If the death becomes impersonal, then so does my salvation. No, I have to be there, at the cross, driving the nails, in order to live now in His salvation. I took His life and, in return, He gave me new life with Him. It's not a concept: it's reality.

Did you kill Jesus?

Acts 2:23, Romans 5:6-8, 1 Peter 2:24, 1 Peter 1:18-19

DECEMBER 3

Text: *Isaiah 21:8: Day after day, my lord, I stand on the watchtower; every night I stay at my post.*

I must be the lion, the watchman, who stands guard over my own soul. When I see the enemy approaching, I must turn to God for protection. A watchman, upon spying danger, alerts the army; he doesn't do battle with the enemy all by himself. I must turn to God for protection when I see the enemy looming on the horizon. I must be ever alert so that the enemy is not able to creep up on me in the night and steal me away from the fortress of God's protection. I must stay awake these hours and days that I have left and pray with God and be alert.

Are you alert?

1 Peter 5:8, Matthew 26:41, 1 Corinthians 16:13, Colossians 4:2

DECEMBER 4

Text: *John 6:12:... Gather the pieces that are left over. Let nothing be wasted.*

The teaching was with loaves and fishes but the words are about men today. The words are about me. I am a leftover. I have been consumed by the world, by my flesh, and by the enemy. My life was being wasted, but there were still some leftover pieces. God is not willing that my life, or the life of any man, be wasted. He came to gather up what was left after this

221

world had had its fill of my body and my soul, and He picked me up and kept me because I am still valuable to Him. God created me; He allowed me to make stupid choices and watched me being eaten up by the enemy. But now He gathers what is left, preserves the crumbs, and makes a whole loaf of me once more.

Will you give what's left to God?

Psalm 34:18, 1 Timothy 1:13-16, Jeremiah 18:4, Matthew 12:24

DECEMBER 5

Text: *Luke 4:13: When the devil had finished all this tempting, he left him until an opportune time.*

Jesus was tempted just as I am tempted, although his temptation was much greater than mine. Jesus was tempted with food when he was starving. I am tempted by appetites that I think I must feed. Jesus was tempted by power to do good. I am tempted by lust for power and glory and honor. Jesus was tempted to take His life into His own hands and to prove His divinity instead of trusting in His heavenly father. I am tempted to abandon my trust in Jesus, the Father and the Holy Spirit, and to do things my own way. Jesus did not give in to any of His temptations. I have given in to all of mine. Satan said that he'd be back. He returned to tempt Jesus, and he will return to tempt me. Lord, keep me safe from the temptation.

How does the enemy tempt you?

James 1:13-15, 1 Corinthians 10:13, Matthew 26:41, Galatians 5:16-18

DECEMBER 6

Text: *Luke 9:23: …If anyone would come after me, he must deny himself and take up his cross daily and follow me.*

I t is hard to deny myself. It is hard to subdue my fleshly desires. It is even harder to pick up my cross, as light as it is. I cannot pick up my cross in my own strength. It is only in the morning as I kneel before Jesus to actually lay hold of the wood and feel the splinters on my hands that I am able to see Jesus there already, ahead of me, waiting to help me pick up my cross. Thank you, Jesus, for helping me today, and tomorrow, and each day thereafter.

Do you carry your cross?
Luke 14:27, Matthew 10:38, Galatians 5:24-25, Philippians 3:7-9

DECEMBER 7

Text: *Luke 19:10: For the son of man came to seek and to save what was lost.*

I was lost. I was in the world and I was so lost that I didn't even know that I was lost. Jesus didn't just call out to me saying, "Here is salvation; come and get it if you want it." Jesus sought me out; he pursued me. Jesus persisted until he found me hiding from Him and gently whispered to me that He loved me. Thank you, Jesus, for loving me enough to find me, even when I didn't want to be found, and then carrying me in your arms to your salvation. I love you, too.

Do you hide from God?
Hebrews 4:13, Psalm 139:7-10, Psalm 90:8, Genesis 3:10

DECEMBER 8

Text: *Leviticus 5:5: When anyone is guilty in any of these ways, he must confess in what way he has sinned…*

T he problem of the penitent, the hurdle that we face, has not changed since the days of Leviticus. It is not just the initial confession, the

223

admission that I have sinned, but it is the dread of admitting my guilt to those that I want to love me, to admire me, and to respect me. The admission, the confession of sin, must not only be made to God but to my brothers and sisters also. Giving the "sin offering" is not nearly as difficult as standing before my loved ones and my brothers and admitting my sin. But God has commanded that I confess and so I must obey. I want the love of my God more than I want anyone else's love, and I am deeply ashamed when I stand before God to confess. But God knows anyway. Help me, Lord, to come before you and your people each time I sin and admit my sin and receive forgiveness.

Are you afraid to admit your sin?
Proverbs 28:13, Ephesians 4:25, James 5:16, Leviticus 5:5

DECEMBER 9

Text: *Deuteronomy 16:3: …so that all the days of your life you may remember the time of your departure from Egypt.*

God commanded his people to set aside a time to remember. They were to remember the time that they had lived in Egypt, lest they be tempted to return. They were to remember the difficulty they had in being set free, and they were to eat unleavened bread to remind them of their headlong flight from their captors. They were to recall leaving all to which they had been accustomed, becoming a vagabond people set aside for God's purpose. They were to remember so that they would never again be tempted and have to repeat the pain of deliverance. My sin is my Egypt. It is good that I remember not that in which I lived, but instead the struggle to be free of my sin, so that I will choose to live with God and without the sin. Help me, Lord, all the days of my life, to remember my struggle and why I fled. Keep my deliverance ever before me.

Do you remember?

Deuteronomy 6:12, Revelation 2:5, Deuteronomy 8:2, Isaiah 46:8-9

DECEMBER 10

Text: *Judges 3:4: They were left to test the Israelites to see whether they would obey the Lord's commands, which he had given their forefathers through Moses.*

When God delivered His people, He left in the land an irritant, a remnant of the enemy, to pluck at the faith of His people. The Israelites had to be tested, lest they forget their deliverance miraculously given to them by the hand of God. Had they lived in God's blessing, without challenge, they would soon forget God's deliverance, and soon forget God. God has delivered me from my sin but remnants of fleshly desire remain. I have prayed for God to take from me these longings. I have been praying for the wrong thing. God has allowed these temptations to remain in my life as proof and a reminder of His miracle. So, Lord, I thank you for what you allow, and I pray that you will give me the strength to obey you in the midst of temptation.

Does temptation remain?

2 Corinthians 12:7-9, 1 Corinthians 10:13, Galatians 5:16-18, James 1:12

DECEMBER 11

Text: *2 Kings 23:26: Nevertheless the Lord did not turn away from the heat of his fierce anger, which burned against Judah because of all that Manasseh had done to provoke him in anger.*

There are consequences of deliberate sin. Manasseh not only sinned deliberately and willfully, but it seems that he took great delight in his sin and rebellion. The consequence was the fierce anger of the Lord. God knows, and I know, that I, too, have sinned, and have sinned deliberately and willfully, even though I took no delight in my rebellion. I know that as a consequence I, too, deserve God's "fierce anger." But God has forgiven me through the sacrifice that Jesus made. I am overwhelmed by God's love for me and His grace.

Do you deserve God's anger?
Romans 2:5-8, Ezekiel 7:8, Romans 6:21-23, 1 John 1:7

DECEMBER 12

Text: *Ezra 10:4: Rise up; this matter is in your hands. We will support you so take courage and do it.*

Ezra, appalled at the sin of God's people, is called to tell them that they must cast away the sin of intermarriage and forsake the children who are the fruit of the sin. Ezra does not want to alienate his people. He loves his people as God loves them, and he doesn't want to do anything that will bring them grief. Elam confronts him and says, "Look! It's your choice about what to do; but you know what God's saying. Be brave! We will back you, but just do it." I am often in the same place with the sin in my life, sin that in many ways, I love. And God says to me, "It's your choice, but you know what I want." I must be brave; God will back me. I must just do it.

Will you choose?

Deuteronomy 30:19-20, Joshua 24:15, Joel 3:14, 1 Kings 18:21

DECEMBER 13

Text: *Job 13:15: Though he slay me, yet I will hope in him.*

I come before God as that which I am: a sinner who deserves to be slain. I admit that I deserve God's judgment, the wrath of His mighty hand, because of my disobedience. But God wants nothing more than my repentance and my true sorrow. He desires to restore fellowship with me: He loves me. I know His love, and I hope in Him. The enemy has been coming against me, and it's so hard for me to stand. Obedience eludes me as I turn my face to Earthly delights and my mind to baubles of the flesh. But God loves me and so I turn to Him, and I hope in Him. Against all odds, God's hand is stretched out, welcoming me.

What do you do about temptation?

1 Corinthians 10:13, James 4:7, Ephesians 6:10-14, Luke 22:39-40

DECEMBER 14

Text: *Job 36:21: Be careful, do not turn to evil; for you have preferred this to affliction. (NASB)*

God has allowed affliction in my life that I might learn. If I come to Him in times of trouble, I learn from Him. I have learned that affliction does not last forever. I have learned that I can see the face of God in the confusion that trouble brings--if I look hard enough. I have also learned that only God can bring me through true affliction. I know, now that if I give up, that if in my pain I turn to sin to make myself feel better, I will become addicted to making myself feel better, and I will not allow God's healing to take place. Thank you, God, for the affliction and the healing you bring about through the pain.

How do you handle affliction?

Psalm 34:17-20, 2 Corinthians 12:9, Romans 8:18, Philippians 4:6-7

DECEMBER 15

Text: *Amos 4:11: You were like a burning stick snatched from the fire, yet you have not returned to me, declares the Lord.*

The hardest part of my sin is my stubborn refusal to be snatched from the fire. I know that I continue to sin, and I also know that God provides a way of escape. I can see God's mighty hand showing me the inevitable consequences of my sin, and I hear his voice prophesying destruction if I remain in my sin. And yet, I persist in sin. Is the pleasure of a moment stolen from God and from my relationship to Him so great that I will continue in my self-imposed destruction? Oh Lord, touch this stubborn man, that I may finally reject ALL the sin in my life.

Will you escape from your sin?

Acts 3:19, Galatians 6:7-8, Romans 6:15-16, Psalm 23:4

DECEMBER 16

Text: *Zechariah 10:12: "I will strengthen them in the Lord and in his name they will walk," declares the Lord.*

I will not be strengthened unless I am strengthened in the Lord. I am not able to walk unless I walk in his name. It will take great courage and incredible strength to walk in holiness and purity in a world filled with impurity and sin. It will take impossible discipline to obey God in this world that is so filled with temptation. I have not the strength, the discipline, the courage, nor the character to succeed in my attempts to be holy. Yet, if I submit to God, he will strengthen me, give me courage, and discipline me for the journey.

Where is your strength?

Exodus 15:2, 2 Timothy 1:7, 2 Thessalonians 3:3, Psalm 20:6-8

DECEMBER 17

Text: *1 Thessalonians 1:4: For we know, brothers loved by God, that he has chosen you.*

If I have chosen Christ, He has chosen me. In fact, He chose me before I chose Him. He chose me to follow Him before time existed, and He chose me for only one reason: He loves me. As I scurry through life, contending with the daily frustrations and temptations, it is sometimes difficult to stop and realize that God still loves me. As I fail, and betray Christ in my sin, it is often hard to recall that I am chosen by God. It is necessary for me to stop, cease my activity, and listen for the voice of the one who loves me, so that He may reaffirm to me that I am indeed chosen, and loved, in spite of my sin and failures.

Do you choose to be chosen?

Isaiah 43:10, Ephesians 1:13, John 6:37, Romans 11:5

DECEMBER 18

Text: *Proverbs 12:1: Whoever loves discipline, loves knowledge, but he who hates correction is stupid.*

Who among us loves discipline? Who does not hate being corrected? Discipline is difficult. It is denying my flesh and the laziness of my soul. It forces me to concentrate on the things in my life that I must do to be healthy--spiritually and physically. It calls me to denial of desire, the desire to play and to be served. Correction strikes at my pride. How many can say that they enjoy being humbled by being proven wrong? The correction often means that I cannot go where I have been going and can no longer do what I have done. Correction is hard and often painful. I do not love discipline, nor do I like correction, but I love the result of discipline, and I love the result of correction. As I am disciplined and corrected, I become closer to God.

Will you be disciplined?

Hebrews 12:11, Job 5:17-18, Psalm 94:12-13, Proverbs 3:12

DECEMBER 19

Text: *Proverbs 14:12: There is a way that seems right to a man, but in the end it leads to death.*

If I act in my own strength and reasoning and listen to worldly wisdom, I will see the world as in a mirror, and my vision is limited to my own reflection. Worldly wisdom, therefore, will guide me in paths that promise pleasure, wealth, and power, for I will be at the epicenter of my own world.

It will be a world that I have created, not the real world that God has created. The ways that I choose would seem to be so good and so right. They promise riches, control over others, and power over my own destiny. They promise immediate gratification and the sating of my lusts. The advice on which I rely is from others who also seek worldly wisdom, that they may have pleasure. For a time, I may be successful and think that my fortune is secure and my future safe, but at the end there will be nothing at all.

Do you choose heaven or Earth?
Isaiah 55:7-8, Proverbs 3:7, John 5:30, Romans 12:2

DECEMBER 20

Text: *Proverbs 15: 26: The Lord detests the thoughts of the wicked, but those of the pure are pleasing to him.*

When I am wicked or evil it is because of my thoughts. Sin is born not in the members of my body, but rather in my mind. My mind controls my body, and my body must obey. Sin starts out in my mind as a suggestion, just a trace of impurity, or greed, or lust. It is small and easily ignored, but it is persistent. Unless I deal with it, in its infancy, it grows and takes root and becomes strong. Even as it grows, I hear myself say, "I would never do that," or, "I won't do that again," or, "I am finished with that." But if I do not uproot the seedling of disobedience in my mind immediately, it blossoms and becomes full grown, and my body obeys the sinful thought. God detests the impure and disobedient thought and so must I. I must think about things that please God for they will please me also.

What are you thinking?
Philippians 4:8, 2 Corinthians 10:5, Ephesians 4:22-24, Psalm 139:23-24

DECEMBER 21

Text: *Proverbs 26:11: As a dog returns to its vomit, so a fool repeats his folly.*

What part of the lesson did I not learn the first time? I was trapped in my sin and had no way out. I became desperate for deliverance. I was weary to the bone, of my slavery to sin, and my soul cried out to be set free. God delivered me from my slavery to sin, a miraculous moment, as all deliverance is miraculous. Then I began the long and arduous task of working out my deliverance. It has not been easy. It has not been without failure, but it has been a steady climb, upward, always upward, and with many joyous moments. I see how far I have come. Do I now desire to go back to the enslavement of sin and start the journey all over again? I am tempted still, but I will not return to the vomit of my past.

Does sin keep pulling you back?
Hebrews 10:26-27, 2 Peter 2:20-21, 1 John 2:15-17, Philippians 1:6

DECEMBER 22

Text: *Proverbs 27:1: Do not boast about tomorrow, for you do not know what a day may bring forth.*

I have done well in my recovery from my enslavement to sexual sin. But sometimes I find myself thinking that it's over, that the enemy can no longer touch me. I must be very careful, for my adversary, Satan, is very smart and very patient. He is a trained and experienced hunter who tracks his prey. He keeps in the shadows so that I will believe I am safe. And when I have stopped looking over my shoulder, when I am no longer afraid that he will overtake me, when I become comfortable in my safety, he will strike from the corner that I least expect. I must not boast, not even to myself, that my rebellion is gone and that I am safe, for the enemy listens with eager anticipation. If I boast because for now the enemy is not found in my life, I must boast only of the mercy of my Lord.

Do you boast of your healing?

Psalm 75:4, Psalm 94:4, 1 Corinthians 1:31, Galatians 6:14

DECEMBER 23

Text: Psalm 3:2: Many are saying of me, "God will not deliver him."

There are some who know of my sin, who say the sin will never be overcome in my life. The world often thinks that this particular sin will never be forgiven. Sometimes I believe the world and find myself agreeing that I will never be free of this besetting sin. But the world lies to me; it is a lie from the pit of hell and the lips of Satan himself. For I have heard the voice of God, and He has told me of His deliverance. He has told me who I am and that He will deliver authority to me, to be free of this besetting sin. My God does not speak that which is not. So even in the face of failure there is deliverance. Even among the taunts and jeers of the world, even in the accusations of my own thoughts, I will stand firm in God's word and I will be delivered.

Can you be healed?

1 Peter 2:24, Psalm 103:2-5, Psalm 30:2-3, James 4:7-10

DECEMBER 24

Text: *Psalm 8:4: What is man that you are mindful of him, the son of man that you care for him?*

I am one single man in the entire universe that God has created, one face in the sea of created peoples. Why does God care what I do? If I sin, or if my father sinned, why does God care one way or the other? There must be so many people, over the ages, that have obeyed God, and I am just one single man standing on the precipice of eternity. Why does God even care about what I do or don't do? It is because of God's great master plan for our world and for all of creation. I, as insignificant as I am, am a part of the plan, necessary to its success. I am an exceedingly small part but vital none-theless. But it's so much more than being a cog in the machinery of eternity. God cares because He loves me. He is my father, and I am His son.

Does it matter if you sin?
Isaiah 59:2, Micah 3:4, Romans 1:21-25, Genesis 3:17-19

DECEMBER 25

Text: *Psalm 27:1: The Lord is my light and my salvation – whom shall I fear? The Lord is the stronghold of my life – of whom shall I be afraid?*

Sometimes I am really afraid: people attack me, circumstances pile up against me, and I become overwhelmed. Sometimes I feel that I don't have the strength to withstand the onslaught of problems, and temptation sneaks in to pull me down into the morass. I sometimes look out and am so discouraged that I see no hope. But then I hear the voice of God as he calls me to give my problems to him so He can guide me through. God doesn't change my circumstances; he changes me. I look up and I see God, strong, fearless, willing to and capable of taking care of me with His mighty hand. I will fear nothing and no one.

Are you afraid?

Isaiah 41:10, Philippians 4:6-7, Psalm 23:4, Jeremiah 29:11

DECEMBER 26

Text: *Psalm 55:6: Oh that I had the wings of a dove! I would fly away and be at rest.*

My God has not created me to flee from the battle, but rather He created me to fight. When I am overcome by the fight and I am weary, it is because I have been carrying the burden of battle rather than trusting God to carry it for me. Even in the midst of a war- torn life God gives me rest and strength to fight anew as I wake and trust Him, as I rely on Him for the victory He has promised. But sometimes I am so weary, and I need a place of comfort and rest. God knows. But even if I did have the wings of a dove, where would I fly? There is no rest in the world, and I would not find rest. God gives me wings, not doves' wings, but God's wings, that I might fly to Him; that I might not find a resting place, but that I will be at rest.

Where is your rest?

Matthew 11:28-30, Jeremiah 31:25, 1 Peter 5:7, John 16:33

DECEMBER 27

Text: *Psalm 110:2: The Lord will extend your mighty scepter from Zion; you will rule in the midst of your enemies.*

We are fallen kings, men who God created to rule the world around us. But the world has defeated us in battle after battle. Sin and temptation have convinced us that we are fallen, and that we have lost the war and been taken captive by an evil world. We live as if in chains, oppressed by sin. But God sees us as rulers. He says stand, be who I created you to be. You are kings of the world; you are my princes. I have delivered you from your captors, broken your chains and clothed you with the royal cloaks of rulers. Now, even now, I will gird you up as I anoint you with my scepter. You are to rule the land that I have given to you. You are to rule in the midst of your enemies, and you are not to be afraid, for I am with you.

Are you God's warrior?

Psalm 144:1-2, Jeremiah 20:11-12, 1 Corinthians 16:13, Joshua 1:9

DECEMBER 28

Text: *Psalm 139:23: Search me, O God, and know my heart; try me, and know my anxious thoughts.*

Lord, you need not search very hard to know my disobedient heart, how my flesh cries out for pleasure. But Lord, you created me to have a pure heart before you, and so I will have a heart that is turned toward you. Lord, examine me perpetually, never cease to watch and to correct my motives as well as what I do. When I stray, when I even begin to stray, stop me Lord and bring me back upon the path you have chosen for me. You know my anxious thoughts, Lord, my deepest fears, the things that make me afraid that I will miss something or that someone else will get my portion. Help me, oh Lord, to see that all my fears are groundless and that they serve no purpose except to keep me from your joy and all that you have for me when my soul is in your hands. Search me, oh Lord, that I may truly be pure before you.

Will you give all your thoughts to God?

Isaiah 26:3, 2 Corinthians 10:5, Colossians 3:2, Romans 8:5

DECEMBER 29

Text: *Luke 22:61: "Before the rooster crows today, you will disown me three times."*
And he went outside and wept bitterly.

There have been so many times that I have been Peter. So often enticed by sin, I have disowned my Lord Jesus and gone willingly, even eagerly, into full-blown sin. Peter wept and, even as Peter, I have wept at my sin, my abandonment of my Lord. But Peter learned; Peter got better. For so long it seemed I would not learn, would be doomed to repeat my folly over and over until I finally grew old and died in my sin. But the Lord has rescued me; He has shown me how to live without denying Him. He has brought me into paths of obedience. I cannot promise God that I will never again deny Him, but I do promise that I will allow His healing in my life. Just as Peter learned, I am learning.

Are you being healed?

Jeremiah 17:14, 1 Peter 2:24, Psalm 103:2-5, Matthew 11:28-29

DECEMBER 30

Text: *Luke 4:12: And Jesus answered and said to him, "It is said, you shall not put the Lord your God to the test." (NASB)*

The temptation that Satan brought was for Jesus to commit a foolish act to prove that God would send His angels to save Him. Satan tempts me in the same way. He presents a temptation to me and then says, "Hey, look at the Scripture. It says God loves you, that He will never leave you or forsake you, that you can confess your sin, this sin, and God will wipe it out of his memory banks." The greater temptation is always to test God, to deliberately enter into sin, to grieve the heart of God, knowing that I will be forgiven if I repent of the sin. That, of course, is the hook, for as I practice this rebellion over and over again, I will not repent, not really, and then Satan will own me. Jesus saw this for what it really was--an invitation to willful sin and, of course, he rejected it. I too must reject Satan's invitation.

Do you test God?

Deuteronomy 6:16, Isaiah 7:12, 1 Corinthians 10:9, Psalm 106:13-15

DECEMBER 31

Text: *Psalm 136: 1&24: Give thanks....to the one who freed us from our enemies, His love endures forever.*

I will give thanks to my God who has led me out of bondage to my sin and my enemies, just as He led Israel out of captivity. As He destroyed Pharaoh's army, so He defeated the power of sin that held me captive. As He provided a way of escape through the desert for Israel, so He provided a way of escape from my sin. As He provided a safe land for Israel, so He has provided a safe place for me. As He provided victory over the enemy in the Promised Land, so He will strengthen me for the battles that are surely before me. As He was faithful to the Israelites, His children, His chosen people, so He has been and will be faithful to me, His son. He protects me and nourishes me because He has chosen me and because He loves me. Your love, O Lord, endures forever.

Are you free?

Galatians 5:1, John 8:36, Psalm 118:5, Romans 8:1-2

ABOUT

KHARIS PUBLISHING

KHARIS PUBLISHING is an independent, traditional publishing house with a core mission to publish impactful books, and channel proceeds into establishing mini-libraries or resource centers for orphanages in developing countries, so these kids will learn to read, dream, and grow. Every time you purchase a book from Kharis Publishing or partner as an author, you are helping give these kids an amazing opportunity to read, dream, and grow. Kharis Publishing is an imprint of Kharis Media LLC. Learn more at https://www.kharispublishing.com.

CPSIA information can be obtained
at www.ICGtesting.com
Printed in the USA
FSHW022258221121

9 781637 460795